# MARBLE ARCH
# MEMORIES

I dedicate this book to my husband, Tommy and our family, Angus, Ishbel and Duncan. Without them there would have been no school, and no tale to tell.

# MARBLE ARCH MEMORIES

By
Jean Macpherson

HYDE PARK SCHOOL CHARITABLE FUND

1st Edition 1992

*Published by*
Marble Arch Memories
27 Archery Close
London W.2

*Copyright*
© Jean Macpherson

*Printed in Great Britain by*

**W. E. BAXTER LIMITED**

34-35 HIGH STREET
LEWES, EAST SUSSEX

ISBN 0 9520709 01

# CONTENTS

# MARBLE ARCH MEMORIES

## FOREWORD

In 1962 Jean Henrietta Stewart Macpherson founded and became Principal of the Hyde Park School in London. Little did she realise it would occupy her working life for the next thirty years.

Jean was educated at Broomfield House School, Didsbury in Lancashire, L'Alpe Fleurie Convent, Villars in Switzerland, St. Clements School, Toronto and Ovendon School, Barrie, Ontario, Canada. On her return to Britain she attended St. Hilary's Church of England School, Alderley Edge in Cheshire and Acton Reynold School near Shrewsbury, followed by teacher training at Moray House and the Edinburgh College of Domestic Science. She is married to Sir Thomas Macpherson CBE MC TD DL and they have three children.

A devout Christian, the author was the first married woman to be appointed an Elder of St. Columba's Church of Scotland, Pont Street, London.

She recounts the joys and heartaches of creating the Hyde Park School. She remembers the pupils who in thirty years have passed through her gifted hands, and the teachers and helpers who to this day remember her with love and affection.

She instigated an Emergency Service which was unique. This enabled children to be looked after between 8 a.m. and 6 p.m. Monday to Friday, fifty two weeks a year. This service has since been adopted in many countries around the world including Russia.

The anecdotes are a joy to read. The stories of challenges and cooperation with Westminster City Council, the Church, the Freeholders, the Neighbours, the Tradespeople and the Community illustrates this fervent Scot's sense of humour, and adventure and her great love of children.

# ACKNOWLEDGEMENTS

This book owes a debt to the Westminster City Council's Library Service for its inspiration: to the support and help of the Hyde Park School staff, pupils and parents from whom many of the stories about the children are drawn; the Rector of St. George's, Hanover Square, the Reverend W.A. Atkins, and Miss Elizabeth Crichton for confirming the historical dates and places.

To Westminster and Inverness Libraries for allowing access for research, and the use of numerous reference books. Mr. Joe Brim and Mr. Gary Duff-Godfrey of Laserbureau Ltd., the fathers of ex-pupils whose expertise designed the book cover and brochure.

To the Cowies, Duffie and Joyce, her brother Robbie Gair and Cathie MacDonald, the quartet who take care of our Highland home and our way of life there. They are the "Guardians of Balavil."

To Mrs. Evelyn Sinclair, Highland Regional Council's Training Organiser of the Jobs, Enterprise and Training Unit for her patience and wise counsel, to Angus Paterson and John Ross for typing and research.

To David Russell of Catercomp for labels rushed out on time, and to Russell and Molly Webb and other collators who searched successfully for photographic references.

To Ian Russell, a fellow Elder of St. Columba's Church of Scotland whose knowledge of grammar and spelling clarified the script.

To Mr. David Cook with Mr. Bob Galli and Mr. John Blackmer of W. E. Baxter Ltd of Lewes, the printers.

# CHAPTER ONE

Post War London was full of left-overs. Left-overs from the bombs of a decade ago, left-overs of multi-owned houses, only half of the occupants traced. Houses part destroyed, part painted, part occupied. Houses waiting to be demolished, houses of great elegance which were unscathed and destined to be survivors.

This area of London in which I lived for the next thirty years was called Connaught Village. When it was built it had been known as Tyburnia. It snuggles cosily between the shops of Oxford Street to the east, and the faded elegance of Lancaster Gate to the west, St. Mary's Hospital, Regent's Canal, Paddington Railway and Police Stations to the north, and to the south Hyde Park.

We are on the "wrong side of the park", but Cockerells' plan for Tyburnia, in the early 1800's, was meant to rectify this. His scheme comprised large stucco houses and a Palladian chapel. His untimely death meant the latter was not completed and George Gutch, the architect who followed him was more practical. On completion, the area was hardly altered until the 1950's.

Our home was one of the few exceptions. In the late 1930's Hyde Park Crescent and Somers Crescent had been rebuilt in red brick. The affluent had flocked in during the Victorian age, but on completion in 1938 our home was unoccupied and at the end of 1939 it was requisitioned as the Headquarters of the Women's Army. After a decade as this it became a place for homeless families and was broken up into tiny apartments. It had then been privately bought, and demolition of the many partitions had begun, when the new owner fell ill and put it on the market again, with the house looking like a battlefield. My husband noticed it as he drove home through the area, saw its possibilities, and bought it there and then.

1

The house was spacious and sunny and was to give us many happy years. We had later on one very odd hiccup. We were living peacefully in Number 10 when suddenly we were notified that the Street was to be totally re-numbered "to correspond with the policy of numbering all streets outward from St. Paul's". This was the decree of the Street Names Department of the late unlamented Greater London Council. There were only twenty houses in our street and at that time about half of them occupied. Every house protested but apparently the bureaucrats had the law on their side and no appeal was possible. So next month we became Number 4, with all the confusion that entails. We were actually the first house in the street which on the even side was logically Number 2, but the officials claimed that on their plans we were actually two houses and Number 2 was dormant.

The ninety-nine year Church Commission Lease of 1934 had insisted it remained as a single family dwelling and by a quickly accepted offer we took possession. It was just as well, as we had broken the agreement on our lease of a spacious flat in neighbouring Hyde Park Square. "No dogs, no children and no prostitutes" was the fatal clause. We wanted the first, had the second and observed at first hand the activities of the third. "Get off my beat" I had been told as I stood on my own front steps awaiting my husband collecting the car from the garage.

The "Red Light" district of Paddington had spread and spread throughout Connaught Village and into Hyde Park. In the sixties, on Sunday walks with Tommy, the children and two Shetland Sheep dogs, we were greeted by many smiling faces, each leaning against one of the old trees in the park. Tommy who has always been a fitness fanatic usually spent an hour running in the park, on the days he was able to be in London, and he saw them so often that he was on first name terms with many of them. Anyway that is his story and he is sticking to it! The House of Commons, the Police and the landlord for this square mile the Church Commissioners, worked hard to bring to an end this social scene, which was motivated by the sale of sex, or the excitement of what used to be, what might have been or what could not possibly have been. The congregations of Great Britain were kept informed by the media and newspapers as many famous names kerb-crawled or negotiated, man to man, woman to woman or some who dressed as either, uncertain of their own gender.

In order to maximise the income from the Hyde Park Estate for the salaries of the Church of England clergy, the Church Commisioners embarked upon constructing high-rise apartment blocks. Building at this time was difficult due to shortages of skilled labour and materials, and the cost of re-housing statutory tenants.

The late 1950's and the early 1960's were years of hope. The neighbourhood could only improve. Tommy liked it for its access to the park and the excellent public transport which would take him to his business and sporting activities and to his beloved Scotland.

Our new home was a roomy flat-chested terraced building, five windows wide and four floors high. The canny Scot I had married liked the well heated homes of our two American neighbours. They helped to save our fuel bills. The shrapnel marked red brick facade needed little maintenance. We fenced in the flat roof so that bagpipes could be played, tri-cycles ridden and gutters and drains could be easily cleared. The back garden was shared with the American Embassy houses and 35 Cambridge Square. We put a door in the wall which led to the communal garden, garage and easy parking facilities for our friends. What more could a family want?

Amid all this dereliction a sense of purpose was return-ing. Families started to buy into the neighbourhood. The elegant Hyde Park Gardens with their stucco exteriors and magnificent interiors were being restored. Original leases dating from Cockerell's time still retained some intriguing clauses relating to communal care of gardens, outside lights and "watches" to be kept day and night for the protection of the garden plants. The streets are wider and airier than fashionable Chelsea and Knightsbridge.

A corner of the estate between Sussex Gardens and Norfolk Crescent was demolished and a luxurious develop-ment called the Water Gardens was built, and completed in 1965, the Porchester Tower in Norfolk Crescent in 1966. In

Hyde Park Crescent one hundred and thirty nine flats were built in three blocks – Castleacre, Southacre and Rainham. It is to be hoped that the Church Commissioners will preserve the village integrity of this conservation area with its listed buildings for decades to come, in spite of population pressure and short term financial goals.

From Marble Arch to Stanhope Place stretch the terraced stucco Georgian houses of Connaught Place, and some brick Victorian replacements. Nineteenth century buildings survive in Stanhope Place, Albion Street, Westbourne Street, and Hyde Park Square. Connaught Square retains nearly all of the brown-brick terraced houses which are rustic in comparison with the nearby Edgware Road.

In our village the fog was less, the air purer than in the lower land south of Hyde Park. We still had the butcher, the baker, the candlestick-maker and a tailor, shoemaker, chemist and a fishmonger too. An advantage of having one landlord is that we knew to whom to turn if development, or re-development queries arose, or if overcrowding became intolerable. New legislation brought freeholds, but the development of our village was now complete. The Minoprio Plan for high-rise homes and small houses had been executed.

In 1967 the former St. George's Hanover Square Burial Ground, of just over two acres, and the site of the bombed Ascension Chapel were purchased by the Utopian Housing Society, who built the flats now called St. George's Fields. They exchanged a five hundred yard strip of land with the Church Commissioners in return for vehicular access into Albion Street. That strip was the builder's yard during the construction period, and was later to become the home of my School.

Like many mothers I had a desire for a roof over my head. Somers Crescent brought much happiness, a bedroom for Angus and the newly arrived Ishbel and one for Joan Marsh, N.N.E.B., their devoted nanny, plus a day and night nursery, kitchen and bathroom all on the top floor. She watched over both children every day with love and affection.

4

Meanwhile I continued teaching teenage girls on the home makers course at the Monkey Club in Pont Street, Chelsea, and at the Quintin Hogg Polytechnic in Regent Street, which in 1992 became the Westminster University. The students and I struggled together to enable them to achieve the City and Guilds 245 Certificate in Home Management.

The great Jesuit priest, Ignatius Loyala, said "Give me a child until it is seven years of age and he will be mine for life". These wise words had been re-inforced during the Catholic period of my upbringing, when I attended L'Alpe Fleurie School in Villars in Switzerland. Delicate health had required me to spend my first two years in a Princess Christian Nursing Home, and asthma precipitated my first overseas journey. I was seven. Now I was faced by the dilemma my mother had had, of giving to another the care of my two most precious possessions. Oh what pain we mothers suffer in the name of progress as we hand over our progeny for education! I was conceited enough to think that no-one could do a better job than I. All it needed was an excellent teacher such as Joan Marsh, Princess Christian trained, my age, and with my ideals. "Read by four years of age and the desire to learn will always remain kindled".

Several friends were already bringing their children whilst they worked, played golf or met their husbands off planes. Blessed with such space, peace, dogs, hamsters, gold-fish, canaries and a garden, we were a self sufficient unit.

No matter what their religion, colour or up-bringing, children need to flourish in confidence and self-expression. Learning this comes easily in a happy, peaceful and orderly routine. A.A. Milne's idea of "it's time to stop for tea" epitomises what a stable and quiet routine all children deserve. With this in mind I embarked on a project which was, to all intents and purposes, to become my life's work for the next thirty years.

# CHAPTER TWO

Joan Marsh came to us as nanny to our first born in 1959 and was known as Nana. She was a beloved member of the family and an inspiration in starting the school. She was born in 1929 and trained at the Princess Christian College, Windsor, tall, thin, wiry with glasses, and an enthusiast about outdoor exercise of every form. She came into our lives just after Angus was born. She was with us for nearly eight years and then moved on just before Lady Redesdale's fifth child, Henrietta Jane was born. I will never forget the day the sixth and next Mitford arrived after five sisters. His father, Clem, 'phoned me at 3 o'clock in the morning saying "You have to get over to the Westminster Hospital right away, we have had a son and I have champagne flowing". In my rather sleepy state I clambered over there and we had the most hilarious party. Lady Redesdale is a very independent person. She does not like having anyone else in her house except for her family and that is plentiful. She added by fostering two boys, James and Paul, the same age as Rupert my godson so he was not brought up in a totally female society.

Lady Redesdale organised a flat at 15 Chalcot Avenue for Nana and she came in daily. This seemed to work much better than having two strong personalities under the one roof. When eventually the youngest child was past the nappy stage, Joan Marsh wanted a move. Before we knew it, she had become nanny to another group of little girls called Samuel. Their father, Nicholas Samuel was the nephew of Lord Bearsted. This was another amazing coincidence. The Samuel family had for long owned a fine grouse moor in Macpherson Clan country, and Dick Bearsted and his lovely wife Heather had become close friends, with frequent week-end visits to their beautiful Warwickshire home, Upton House. When Dick died, my husband Tommy was invited to be the speaker at his synagogue memorial service. He found it a terrifying experience but considered his choice, by Dick's daughter, Felicity, to be perhaps the greatest compliment he had ever been paid. How strangely fate can inter-twine us! Nicholas married Caroline, a doctor, from a very Orthodox Jewish family, and Joan Marsh went to live with them at 18 Loudon Road. They had one daughter after another, until the fifth was a boy, as indeed did his brother, Michael, who had three daughters before he had a son. Joan Marsh worked for them until retiring in 1991 to her home in Dawlish, in Devon, and celebrated by breaking her hip. She used to take the children there for holidays and always had one or two Macphersons or Mitfords with her. Now she has the luxury of peace.

When Angus was two, a few mothers and I decided to join together at Somers Crescent. We had plenty of space for a nursery, a large roof garden and, at the rear, an enclosed garden which was safe and spacious. Nana and I became very friendly with the Paddington Council Health Visitor, Miss MacLeod, a fellow Scot, who hailed from the Western Isles. The opportunity to grow into an organised group came unexpectedly. Miss MacLeod ran the London County Council's Public Health Service Clinic in St. John's Church Hall, over which we looked, and after many applications she was offered new premises in Lisson Grove. She suggested we take on the remainder of the lease, so several friends' nannies could meet, share the time-table and allow everyone a day off.

On March 2nd 1962 I met the Reverend Ivor Lewis at his beautiful Vicarage, a large Georgian building, damaged beyond repair by a bomb which fell between it and the church. He was soon to retire. The lease, which little did I know, had been condemned by the Public Health Department because of a fracture in the sewage pipe, was willingly handed over and I was sent to the Parish Church of St. James's, Sussex Place for finalisation. Prebendary George Chappell was the interim caretaker whilst the Benefice of St. John's Church was vacant and the Bishop of London was thinking about the Church's future. A more charming and helpful ally I could not find. "Take the south side gardens and the vaults beneath for storing the larger toys. Use the main entrance to the hall and keep the school equipment under the stairs to the vestry. All is unused and the vital papers of the premises are up there so you will act as an extra deterrent to closure". He added "Pay a little now and more when and if you can". I took on the three years remaining of the lease conditional upon fulfilling regulations on April 1st 1962, and this was witnessed by the Rt. Hon. Lord Lisle and Colonel Luke Dimsdale.

Excitement mounted as we sought decorators, plumbers and electricians. "You'll know every civil servant in London before you're off the ground" Mr. John P. Hollamby A.R.I.C.S. cheerfully said, as on May 10th 1962 as Manager of the Hyde Park Estate for Chestertons he confirmed that the Church Commissioners raised no objections. On the contrary, they agreed there was a need, and actively encouraged George Chappell to persuade the Bishop to grant a licence. The London County Council Town and Country Planning Act 1947-59 displayed for one to see if I wished to trek across the River Thames to look at it in North Block, County Hall, S.E.1., granted on July 6th 1962 permission to the Metropolitan Borough of Paddington's Director of Housing, 2 Howley Place, London W.2. Permit No 133 to have St. John's Church Hall used as a Nursery School. This was but the beginning, Permit No.105 granted the above on September 13th 1962 by the Paddington Borough Council Health Department. The follow-on was the arrival of Dr. Moss-Morris, from the Somers Town Welfare Centre, Ossulston Street, the medical inspector sent by Leslie Oldershaw, the Divisional Medical Officer from the London County Council's Division 2 Health Office at 313 Harrow Road on September 9th 1962, which led to Day Nursery Registration on October 9th 1962 and we even got a London Fire Brigade Certificate from Albert Embank- ment S.E.1. Surely now we were out of the woods of bureaucracy but no. Mr. W.H. Beubly, Town Clerk and Solicitor of the Metropolitan Borough of Paddington, Town Hall, Paddington Green, W.2. under the Town and County Planning Act 1947, General Development Order 1950, had been delegated authority by the London County Council to grant permission to use part of the hall at St. John's for children. Mr. Oldershaw granted a Registration for twenty places of 3-5 years old children on January 1st 1963 under the Child Minders Regulation Act. Under the Amendment Act the Registration granted an extension for thirty two children after further inspection by Dr. S.M. Morris. What a procedure!

Mr. Weinman of Kininmonts, the local builders, had been returning Somers Crescent to civilisation and undertook the task of the alterations, but it was an expensive business. We lived on the top floor while building work went on in the rest of our house. At Ishbel's christening party (she had been born in July), conducted by Dr. Moffat, on November 27th 1960 in Crown Court Church of Scotland, Covent Garden, where my brother-in-law Niall Lord Drumalbyn was an Elder, and his uncle before him, we used for the first time the ground floor. Her godparents were Diana Strathcarron, wife of Tommy's cousin David, Freddie Cardozo, a close army friend of my husband's from a family deep in the "Latin Mass" tradition of the Roman Catholic Church, and Dr. Meg Ercolani, a Scot, who had been a kind neighbour a year earlier when I mis-carried and deposited a future Macpherson in the car park of the local Cricket Club whilst a match was in progress. Christopher Chataway and Count André de Limur accepted as the other two godfathers to look after the spiritual welfare of this lively lass. André I had first met through mutual friends some time earlier and we had become instant friends. He was a highly cultured and intellectual Frenchman, much older than me, whose family home was the ancient Chateau de Limur in Brittany. A frequent visitor to London, he was now resident in California where he had married the daughter of the subsequently ill-fated Crocker Bank. Alas, this charming man died prematurely, a very sad loss to Ishbel and to me. Christopher Chataway is still in the best of health. He and Tommy had been associated with athletics, as members of Achilles, the Oxford – Cambridge University Athletics Club. Christopher was younger than my husband, so that they were not "up" at Oxford together. It was on the athletic track that they first met, at Aldershot before we were married, where at the same meeting Chris in his first big public race as a National Service man won the Army mile, and Tommy in his last ever race won the T.A. mile.

A few years later, in 1954 at our Hyde Park Square flat's lovely big drawing room we had a summer evening party for athletic friends, as a send-off to Achilles colleagues who were heading for the Commonwealth Games in Vancouver. Chris Chataway was there and Chris Brasher, later Olympic Gold Medallist in Melbourne and Roger Bannister and several others. Roger, first four minute miler, who won the famous race in Vancouver against the great Australian John Landy, had been a particular protégé of Tommy's at Oxford.

All this talent went out through the big French windows into the warm summer evening air on the balcony, overlooking the Square, and partied noisily and happily. Next morning we received in the post a letter from our distant landlord saying that they had forgotten to mention that the balcony was due for repair and was unsafe for more than one person at a time. England nearly did not have a team at Vancouver!

Chris Chataway became a Cabinet Minister and Privy Counsellor, then proceeded to a major career in banking, whilst Roger Bannister, knighted for his services to sport is now in the enviable position of Master of an Oxford College – Pembroke.

Andrew Stainton was a Dewar of the great whisky family, on his mother's side. An enormous man of great affability, he married a tiny but beautiful Greek, Mikaela Likiardopoulos. They moved into the flat upstairs when we lived on the first floor of 16 Hyde Park Square. They were super neighbours, of great charm and humour. Mikaela once boasted that in minutes she could capture the attention of any man. For a bar of chocolate I challenged her with my older bachelor brother-in-law, a surgeon, who was staying the night with us. She appeared, quite stunning in a tight silver lamé top, sleek black velvet trousers, and white fur slippers with very high heels. "Archie darling" she huskily murmured, "I've heard so much about you and I need your advice so

11

badly" as she sat down very close to him on the sofa, "about my constipation". I lost my bar of chocolate.

Now two years later with the Somers Crescent house barely completed we were embarking with our competent builders again. Financially to make ends meet was a big headache but the house was very adaptable. Malinee Pramualratana, the teenage daughter of our Embassy neighbours joined the family as her own parents had returned to Thailand. Malinee's mother I had met at a ladies' diplomatic party, and finding that we lived close together, she asked to come and see me. There she explained in her far from fluent English that her husband was a General at the Embassy, of a distinguished family and much travelled, but she had never been outside Thailand before and was very worried about how to entertain Western diplomats. So we got out the silver and glass, and sitting cosily on the carpet before a roaring fire (no smoke-free zone then) we laid out formal dinner places. Subsequently Tommy asked her husband how the first important dinner had gone. The answer was perfectly – except that it was all laid out on the carpet! Later we became good friends, and Malinee was a delightful member of the family.

Sue and Robert Stinson, a lawyer and teacher and an athletic friend of Tommy's university days, moved into the basement as they had returned from honeymoon to find themselves without a home. Their promised new house was running months late in completion. Instead of rent, they painted and cleaned the flat and made it thoroughly habitable – no mean feat as Robert was in plaster from foot to hip with a torn Achilles tendon, but I know no more talented and determined pair. He has given a lifetime of work to athletics, to the Achilles Club and to Great Britain and the International Athletic Federation of which he is now Treasurer, respected throughout the world.

Books of expenditure recorded every penny spent, laboriously written up by me in the evenings, as Tommy was frequently away on business. At this time he was also commanding the London Scottish Regiment and having his portrait painted by Mr. Egerton Cooper. Egerton Cooper was then President of the Portrait Painters Society and like many in those days of truly penal taxation was not interested in the strain of highly paid portrait painting once he had earned enough. But he loved his art, and for his own and his students' benefit he first painted me, head only, and then a full length of Tommy with kilt and gun, in typical pose, all for the cost of frame, canvas and the right to hang it at the Royal Academy later that year. His barn-like studio in Chelsea was extraordinary, full of fascinating things he had painted in his long career, apparently just for his own satisfaction. He took us to the President's Box at what proved to be the last of the old traditional Chelsea Arts Balls at the Albert Hall. It lived up to its name as colourful, rowdy, boisterous and great fun. The central feature, a pretty mermaid, soon lost her tail, but it was all without violence or malice.

My husband introduced me to a professional team of friends and helpers to guide me through the intricacies of starting a school and our partnerships lasted until its sale. The team consisted of people who really took a personal interest. There was Hamish Easdale, an accountant whom we knew at the London Scottish Rugby Club, and who on retirement handed me over to his splendid and patient Australian partner, Peter Sherring, still our prop and stay. He never denied the facts in my account book were correct but clearly became a little irritated when red numbers in the bank statement caused him to pick up the phone and say "Stop!" I found myself permitted only to sign wages cheques each Friday unless he rang to say more was in the kitty. There was John Fleming, a lawyer whom we had both known, prior to our marriage, willing to divert from the great city world of Stephenson Harwood to give time to our little enterprise, and Peter Kininmonth, the insurance giant. Indeed Peter is a giant in every aspect, a very large man with a still larger personality. He had been an Oxford rugby colleague of Tommy's and though he opted for Richmond rather than London Scottish for excellent reasons which later led to his marriage, he became a popular and successful Captain of Scotland. His abounding energy has given him great business success. In later years he introduced Tommy to one of his most important American contacts, giving my husband an

enduring transatlantic business link that he has much enjoyed. He and his lovely wife, Priscilla remain among our
favourite people. Insurance for premises and children and
staff was a source of major consideration. The lease for
Somers Crescent, being Church Commission, tied us to
Ecclesiastical Insurance. We found their charges demon-
strably and increasingly out of line, and after years of protest
we were allowed the alternatives of Legal & General or
Lloyds. The other school premises and liabilities were generally covered by Eagle Star, whose Chairman's daughter
Georgina Mountain was a friend of Ishbel at the French
Lycée.

I continued to teach at the Monkey Club, two days a
week and carried out regular supply work at the Quintin Hogg
Polytechnic, Greycoats School and the Sacred Heart Convent
at Hammersmith.

It was such a pleasure to have a home after the nomadic
life between our eviction from the Hyde Park Square flat on
Angus's birth in 1958, and our arrival in Somers Crescent in
1960. Nana and the children frequently went to her parents in
Dawlish or to a cottage on my husband's boss's estate at
Woodford Green belonging to Sir Stuart Mallinson where we
all camped for a longer than expected time.

Sir Stuart, a larger than life character, was to become
my twin sister's father-in-law. He kindly included us in his
many interesting activities. His home was on the edge of Sir
Winston Churchill's constituency and the White House became his election base.

Churchill and Field Marshal Montgomery became
great friends to us and indeed earlier we had spent the final
weekend of our honeymoon with Monty. "I have put a guard
outside your bedroom door to stop the men getting ideas. I
never have before had a woman staying here at the Chateau
de Courance" (the SHAPE Headquarters). We had separate
bedrooms. "Should you wish to visit your husband go via the
balcony". The twinkle in his eyes said it all. The next day he
brought to the lunch table his wedding gift to me, a beautiful
large bottle of Chanel No.5 with a massive glass stopper. The
reverse of the norm in everything he did, he tore off the

wrapping, undid the ribbon and tried to open the bottle. It was awkward for fingers inexperienced in ladies' trinkets, so the fourth person present, his A.D.C., was instructed to produce a bucket of hot water and one of ice. The bottle was plunged from one to the other to ease the stopper. At last victory was his, it opened suddenly and emptied a large part of the contents on himself. Shortly afterwards he was summoned to receive garden party guests. I have often wondered what the distinguished visitors thought. "It will keep the mosquitoes away" was Monty's only comment.

It was a great delight to reminisce with him years later about Angus for whom with his sister the School was started. He gave me courage when I felt we would never find a permanent home, and continued to encourage and visit my venture when I started the School. He liked the idea of the Church Hall. His strict Christian ethics never left him nor his devotion to Angus. I often wonder if Angus was subconciously influenced by the words Montgomery wrote to us. He had promised years before that he would guarantee peace for fifteen years from 1958. Now he wrote that his prophecy had been fulfilled, and "It is now up to Angus to become a soldier and carry on the task of preventing war when I have passed over Jordan".

When Angus was born on the nineteenth of December 1958 at the Westminster Hospital in London, my husband announced in the papers that "Angus Cameron Stewart Macpherson whilst maintaining his Scottish domicile was born in London". Our Scottish roots have always been a very important factor in our lives. He was christened at St. Columba's Church of Scotland in Pont Street by the Very Reverend R.F.V. Scott, a former Moderator of the General Assembly of the Church of Scotland. All our three children have one continental godparent and his is Prince Michel de Bourbon-Parme. His godmothers are Heather Bearsted who is now Lady Grierson, and my twin sister, Councillor Anne Mallinson. Ian Fairhurst, the architect, was the other godfather.

From Hyde Park School, he went to Hill House School, in Hans Crescent, brilliantly run by Stuart Townend known to all as The Colonel. He was an ex-Oxford and international half-miler who knew my husband through the Achilles Club and as our friendship ripened over the years he gave me invaluable, and at times unconventional advice for my school. Remembering Angus's days at Hill House brought to mind an incident. One day when I went to collect him from school I was welcomed by all in Hans Crescent looking up at the handsome corner Victorian building in which the school is located and saw that two young gentlemen aged six and a half years had climbed out of a third floor window, their rust coloured corduroy shorts and golden sweaters clearly to be seen in the sunlight. Calmly a stern Colonel Stuart Townend was instructing them on a suitable return route of a less dangerous nature. Angus Macpherson and Charlie Kirwan-Taylor were retrieved and released home only after a thorough washing and reprimand. As the dogs played in the park on the way back joined by Ishbel in the pram I asked Angus what had inspired them. "We'd decided we would be window cleaners and that's how they clean windows – at the top floor at home". His imagination carrying him away with the same enthusiasm caused his first school essay to be entitled "The Purple Headed Stag". "The Stag is a Daddy Deer. At my home in Scotland they all have purple heads as they eat so much heather." Despite these events Colonel Townend and his staff gave Angus an excellent start and I was miserable when my husband decreed that he should go north to his old prep boarding school, Cargilfield in Edinburgh, at seven and half years of age.

My sister-in-law, Sheila Macpherson married Dinks Kittermaster an Oxford and England rugby player, and he was the headmaster of that school from 1940 to 1965. His successor, whom Angus liked and respected, was K.L.T. Jackson, also a rugby man, in his case Oxford and Scotland. In his first winter term, Angus had his ear badly torn. The school notified us and I sent him cards and various bits and pieces. My husband firmly said "do not go up and visit him. You are being a bothersome mother, mothers don't interfere at prep school". I waited until Christmas, when he burst into tears and said "Why didn't you visit me when I had my sore ear, all the other boys had their mothers visit them". It was the last time I did not allow my natural instincts to be the primary mover.

He had been registered for Eton. The Vice-Provost Fred Coleridge came north and stayed in Newtonmore every summer. We got to know him and Julia his lovely and artistic wife. We were fortunate enough to attend a small private dinner where we had the opportunity to meet Mr. Chenevix Trench, the headmaster of Eton and his wife. This able, highly intelligent, and very amusing man charmed us all, but on the way home I said to my husband "I give in, you may send him to Fettes in Edinburgh because I feel as a headmaster, Mr. Chenevix Trench is quite excellent, but he is not right for Angus, a tall willowy gentle soul who will probably be looking after the needy rather than getting on with his 'O' levels and 'A' levels exams, which I think is probably what his future requires". Then came the hiccup. In four hundred years of the existence of Eton as a school, no headmaster had ever left it to go to another school, but Mr. Chenevix Trench left Eton for Fettes. This piece of information reached us at the beginning of the summer term just before Angus was due to go. On hearing this, I rang Fred Coleridge and asked for his advice. He remembered my letter withdrawing him. Subject to him passing the special entrance exam, Angus would have a place at Eton. The exam was due the next day, the appointed date for all Eton applicants. I rang Cargilfield and asked them if Angus would be permitted to sit. They said yes, if I had the papers there by 9 a.m. I drove to Eton, collected the papers and drove through the night to Edinburgh. I arrived just in time. Angus sat and passed, and spent his academic career at Eton. He enjoyed a marvellous, wide education there, together with lots of rugby and cricket. He went on to Christ Church, Oxford and read engineering.

He left Eton a few days before his eighteenth birthday and decided to fill his "gap" year with worldwide travel and experience. He set out in January 1977 with his cousin Andrew Macpherson, to go overland to Singapore, en route to Australia. I briefly describe elsewhere their epic journey. In Singapore, they sold the van and separated, Andrew having recovered from a nasty bout of dysentry, contracted in Madras and requiring hospital treatment in Kuala Lumpar where they were much helped by the Whitakers, friends of my husband. Andrew went on to Perth, Australia and more training in photography, while Angus bussed and hitched through Indonesia before crossing to Australia, where eventually he descended on our very good friends, the Websters in Melbourne. They were immensely kind throughout his stay there. After a week's blissful idleness, Avril Webster got him working on the "jobs vacant" advertisements, and he was soon employed at the Melbourne Hilton, with a tiny shared flat in town. He graduated from the lowest of the low up to room service waiter and recalls interesting moments, including finding a prominent Australian who had called for midnight champagne naked with two ladies in his bed, and a rather senior Englishman, known to Angus by sight, having breakfast in bed with a lady who was not his wife.

Angus's flat-mate proved to be a drug user, and absconded with all of his savings. Angus is phlegmatic, and just took it as one of life's lessons. He started to save again, and in due course set out to go round Australia. A temporary job in Adelaide, then to the opal mines then another job in Perth. Between the two, on the long train journey, he was lured into a poker school by "pros" and won! The opal experience he will never forget. Andamooka and Cooper Pedy are outposts in the middle of the vast Australian desert, and it is so hot that many of the dwellings are underground, even the pub. Old timers and new venturers scrape and scrape the rocky sand in the hope of finding a fortune. He brought me home a lovely opal, though he did not find any sizeable stones himself.

After a spell in Perth, recouping his finances, he set off north, first stop Hammersley, the iron ore town many hundreds of miles away. In due course he got a lift in a huge dumper truck. After a bit, the driver said "I'm tired, you drive". Angus had never even sat in such a vast machine, but as the driver went instantly to sleep there was nothing for it but to try, and thus he arrived triumphantly at Hammersley. Fortunately there had been no traffic on the road. From there, a series of lifts took him to the vast distances round the coast to Broome and beyond, until one day his lift dropped him at the only junction they had seen. The driver was going south to a sheep station, and Angus on to Darwin. "Bye mate, someone will come along in an hour or two". Over twenty four hours later a car came by and picked up one burnt and dehydrated traveller. Angus was taken to a hospital at the next town, a long way off, and there he slept like a log in an iron cot that was so much too short for his six foot four inch slender figure that in his sleep he rubbed both heels raw. It was in that state that he eventually reached Melbourne and met up with his father, who was there on business, and had lots of hot baths and large meals. Undeterred he went on to the United States of America where among other gainful occupations he worked as municipal gardener in Albany, New York. He did not know a rose from a cauliflower! With his American-at-Eton friend, Giles MacNamee, from Boston, he then bought a three hundred dollar jalopy which they drove across to California and back and sold it for $250.

Angus had already met the girl he was destined to marry, and his future mother-in-law, Marigold MacRae of Conchia, met him in Australia in the hot Victoria summer. She met him on his nineteenth birthday in an old Barbour jacket and cord trousers wandering through the Melbourne streets as though he was back in the hills of his beloved Scotland. Valerie Anne MacRae is the fourth of five beautiful daughters of Johnny MacRae, High Constable of Eilan Donan. She was at St. Leonard's School in St. Andrews at that time.

Oxford was a marvellous time for Angus, as it is for everyone, and at Christ Church he savoured it to the full. Clubs, college and university sport. He won his "Greyhound" colours, and was a reserve for the University XV, and elected to Vincents and Gridiron Clubs. He had a very lovely cottage at Shotover during his year of living out, and this was the greatest fun.

He was uncertain what to do after Oxford University and particularly as he had been delayed a year. A broken leg received when playing football against a rowing team at

19

midnight fractured both bones in his right leg in man to man contact. When they carried him off the field to the Radcliffe Memorial Hospital in Oxford, he was seen by a nurse who bade him wait a minute as the Professor of Orthopaedic Surgery was just finishing a long operation. The surgeon walked in the door and said "Angus what are you doing here?" It was Professor Robert Duthie, Angus's first cousin by marriage. Robert put it in plaster from January until June. The pair of them got into a real muddle about Angus's degree finals because both of them could have avoided this problem. Robert knew the finals were about that time but had not linked the amount of pain that happens to a person who has a plaster removed after so long a spell. Angus, who could have given him the exam dates, had the plaster removed in the morning and sat an exam in the afternoon. He could not concentrate because of the pain. The next day he came in doped to the eye-balls and he could not sit his second paper on the Tuesday. On the Wednesday, Thursday and Friday he sat and passed these subjects. He had to re-sit all the exam papers twelve months later.

Whilst waiting he sensibly extended his experience by working in London in the City, six months with the merchant bank, Kleinwort Benson of which his famous Scottish rugby international uncle "G.P.S." had been chairman, and four months with stockbrokers Hoare Govett.

Angus elected to go into the Scots Guards after obtaining his degree. At that time there had been an amalgamation between the Queen's Own Cameron Highlanders, his father's regiment, and the Seaforths, and this put Angus off from opting for them. I loved seeing Angus, as Ensign, carrying the Colour along The Mall to St. James's Palace, then as subaltern in charge of the Buckingham Palace detachment, then as a Major commanding the ceremonial guard at St. James's the prestigious Right Flank, in 1991. I had made a decision that I would like to have Angus photographed in his ceremonial dress uniform, since it might be the last time he would wear it. Angus's contemporary Nick Barlow, who had taken over the post as official School photographer from cousin Andrew, was abroad for six months. The local shop

**HYDE PARK CRESCENT NURSERY – JULY 1963**

*Back Row:* Angus MacPherson, James Trumper, Caroline Rae, Louise Cutner, Punch Hyde-White, David Irving, Erik Lind.

*Middle Row:* Jonathan Cooke, Jane Landau, Julian Williams, Iris Lind, Emma Mitford, Anthony Delarue, Julian Grovenor, Anna Pallant, Katherine Bressler.

*Front Row:* Juliette Hyde-White, Ishbel Macpherson, Tessa Mitford, Simon Huggins, Christopher Bowen, Wendy Vos, Jane Lipert, Maria Marsella.

**HYDE PARK CRESCENT NURSERY – JULY 1964**

*Back Row:* Andrew Macpherson, Jane Landau Angus Macpherson, Amanda Cooper, Julian Williams, Ishbel Macpherson, Justin Stratton-Christiansen, Jane Lipert, Antony Delarue.

*Middle Row:* Adam Rogers, Wendy Vos, Simon Sessler, Maria Masella, Jocelyn Tennant, Helen Macolm, Christopher Gregory, Jane Cutner, Richard Collero.

*Front Row:* Caroline Rodrigues, Sara Baig, Nicole Allen, Nicholas Bresler, Louise Cutner, Christopher Bowen, Susan Galberg, Katherine Bresler, Catherine Rodrigues.

**HYDE PARK CRESCENT NURSERY – MAY 1965**

*Back Row:* Louise Saturninus

*1st Row:* Simon Sessler, William Rollason, Nicole Allen, Steven Lewis, Victoria Louise Mitford, Ian Armstrong, Jocelin Tennent, Simon Savarese, Jeremy Cearns.

*2nd Row:* Cardia Lutyens, Nicole Pallant, Sheila Mallinson, Amanda Harris, Harriet Posner, Kate Mitford, Sara Baig, Helen Malcolm, Sarah Ambrose, Nicole Tinero, Anna Menmuir.

*3rd Row:* Nicholas Bresler, Andrew Impey, Simon Davie, Justin Stratton-Christensen, Stephen Drane, Richard Collero, Richard Gardner-Brown, Dominic Lutyens, Mark Phillips, Martin Young-Taylor.

*Front Row:* Jonathan Cape, Gavin Sasson, Edward Donne, Daniel Kottnauer, Sebastian Gorst.

## HYDE PARK CRESCENT NURSERY – MAY 1966

*Back Row:* Justin Stratton-Christen, Clare Bardsley.

*1st Row:* Jonathan Cape, Amanda Harris, Steven Drane, Kate Mitford, Dominic Lutyens, Victoria Louise Mitford, Andrew Hanson, Helen Malcolm, Jeremy Cearns.

*2nd Row:* Nicholas Bressler, Sara Baig, Martin Young-Taylor, Andrew Impey, Nicole Pallant, Sarah Ambrose, Richard Collero, Sheila Mallinson.

*3rd Row:* Mark Goater, Victoria Richards, Charles Harris, James Griffin, Gillian Lusty, Amanda Ball, Sebastian Gorst, Polly Jane Stainsby, Benjamin Freeman, Anna Menmuir.

*4th Row:* Neil Inglis, Nicole Tinero, Tina Fedeski, Christopher Young-Taylor, Rodolfo Barros, John Melamid, Anne Bricto, Matthew Harris, Anne Germing.

*Front Row:* Helena Tx Ree, John Fedeski, Julian Harvey, Edward Donne, Luke Simkin, Edward and Richard von Abendorff, Candia Lutyens, Aaron Forbes, Patrick Sieff.

## HYDE PARK CRESCENT NURSERY – MAY 1967

*Back Row:* Sarah Sanderson, Ben Lousley Williams, Sara Trumper, Andrew Howland, Louisa Vivian Jane Mullins, Aaron Forbes, Rima Te Wiata.

*2nd Row:* Patrick Sieff, Georgia Horler, Nicholas Lawson, James Griffin, Victoria Richards, Edwin Richards, Charles Harris, Victoria Louise Mitford, Nicolas Stanley-Jones.

*3rd Row:* Tarquin Gorst, Basi Akpabio, Edward von Abendorff, Markham Hanson, Richard von Abendorff, Donald Ingham, Michael Mitchell, Matthew Harris, John Melamed, Mark Mullins, Mona Osman.

*4th Row:* Amanda Ball, Jan Paul Young-Taylor, Anne Berry, Caroline McTear, Jackie Horler, Gigi Goslinga, Fiona Stewart, Gillian Lusty, Lucy Ralston, Lucy Shand Kydd, Mark Pelham, Serena Holley, Anne Goater.

*Front Row:* Sophie Swiney, Danielle Tinero, Henry Hainault, Imogen Cohen, Robin Russell, Jessica Tooth, Anne Brichto, Natasha Hughes.

## HYDE PARK CRESCENT NURSERY – MAY 1968

*Back Row:* Robin Russell, Gigi Goslinga.

*1st Row:* Mona Osman, Patrick Sieff, Anne Berry, Emma-Louise Glascoe, Mark Servaes, Alex Goldsmith, Angus Macdonald, June Matsunobe.

*2nd Row:* Sarah Sanderson, Sarad Thapa, Penelope Harley, Serena Donne, Edwin Richards, Michaella Mitchell.

*3rd Row:* Ann Goater, Sophie Swiny, Henry Hainault, Andrew Budden, John Brown, Natasha Hughes, Joanna Impey, James Cullen, Sophia Wigram, Cybele Cleveland, Jan-Paul Young-Taylor, Gillian Lusty, Tarquin Gorst, Fenella Fox, Markham Hanson.

*4th Row:* Imogen Cohen, Danielle Tinero, Serena Holley, Beth Pollard, Sunitha Nesaratnam, Jessica Forbes, Annabel Lord, Lucy Ralston, Victoria Bennett, Charlotte Stanley-Jones, Robert Sasson.

*Front Row:* Kate Glascoe, Jolyon Luke, Ursula McCarthy, Carolin Beindorff, Marcus Lutyens, Tom Judson, Helen Brown, Simon Sieff, Sarah Harvey, Polly Ann Ball, Ian Cullen, Andrew MacDonald, Deborah Bradstock, Paula Stein, Simon Goodrick, Lynette Marquart.

**HYDE PARK CRESCENT NURSERY – MAY 1969**

*Back Row:* Natasha Hughes, Sarad Thapa.

*1st Row:* Fiona Hardy, Hiroshi Kataoka, Kate Glascoe, Jolyon Luke, Penelope Harley, Rupert Stratton.

*2nd Row:* Serena Holley, Tom Judson, Fenella Fox, Robert Sasson, Danielle Tinero, Marcus Lutyens, Annabel Lord, Carolin Beindorff.

*3rd Row:* Suzette Swiny, Andrew Rothgiesser, Jonathan Sieff, Debbie Bradstock, Simon Sieff, Laura Loudon, Michaella Mitchell, Paula Stein, Fodil Ramoul, Louise Moudari, Jason Massot.

*4th Row:* Ursula Macarthy, Simon Goodrich, Hope Brady, Lynette Marquart, Beth Pollard, Mark Baretto, Eman Abu Zeid, Jason Lewis, Alexandra Watts, Morgan Watts.

*5th Row:* Mary Fabricant, Robert Gordon, Sarah Harvey, Jonathan Foreman, Ann Byner, Sasha Newley, Sarah Bryant, Jonathan Freedman, Susan Gaetz, Paul Hardy.

*Front Row:* Heidi Vaardal, Margaret Berry, Roland Mallinson, Tina Whitmore, Philip Berlin, Lisa Hughes, Eric Libock, Debbie Cooper, Nicola Beindorff, Justine Gonshaw.

## HYDE PARK CRESCENT NURSERY – MAY 1970

*Back Row:* Rick Kelly, Rupert Stratton, Maximilian Wigram, Laura Birnhak, Alexandra Konialidis, Jonathan Lee, James Gordon, Richard Travarelli.

*2nd Row:* Robert Gordon, Camilla Sim, Sacha Newley.

*3rd Row:* Mark Gilrain, Heidi Vaardal, Kevin Gilrain, Heather Keefe, Roland Mallinson, Juliette Hohnen, Jonathan Freedman.

*4th Row:* Anne-Marie Ranson, Rupert English, Isabelle Vieira, Andrew Rothgiesser, Susan Gaetz, Mark Barretto, Suzette Swiny, Jonathan Sieff, Anne Byner, Morgan Watts, Inger Kuhne, Mona Ismail.

*Standing:* Rosalie Enverga, Lisa Hughes, Andrew Weir, Allison Moss, Charles Berger, Camilla Wigram, Austen Kopley, Justine Gonshaw, Lucy Wigram, George Magaronis, Alexandra Watts, David Vorringer, Francesca Patel, Nania Hernandoz.

*Sitting:* Julia Griffin, Elisabeth Forssander, Susuma Karaoka, Marcus Bluett, Claire Hammond, Heidi Joseph, Bettina Hohnen, Kay Montgomery, Julia Cope-Thompson.

*Front Row:* Lucy Potter, Aage Dervas, David St George, Rupert Lord, Anthony Vrondissis, Rupert Mitford, Giles Dunn.

## HYDE PARK CRESCENT NURSERY – MAY 1971

*Back Row:* Maximillian Wigram, Allison Moss.

*2nd Row:* Jonathan Lee, Inger Kuhne, Zeffriali Yusof, Anne-Marie Ranson, Rupert Mitford, Ann Byner, Andrew Weir, Anna Darvas, Jonathan Sieff.

*3rd Row:* Anthony Vrondissis, Cara Pressman, Marcus Bluett, Lucy Wigram, Georgina Mitford, Camilla Wigram, Rupert Lord, Lisa Hughes.

*4th Row:* Sabina Mruck, Mark Longhurst, Alexandra Badger, Susuma Karaoka, Charlotte Martell, Etienne Bourgeois, David St. George, Rebecca Bunyan, Giles Dunn, Victoria Stratton.

*5th Row:* Heather Kelly, Devang Jhaveri, Annabel Eker, James Hamilton, Sacha Llewellyn, Emma Bourne, Annabel Frost, Alexander Mackenzie, Yoko Noguchi, Rodrigo Marquez, Irina Cleveland, Jonathan Hynes, Deborah Stone.

*Front Row:* Lisa Joseph, Carlos Dominguez, Amanda Foreman, Robert Harley, Penelope Gonshaw, Sean Vaardal, Nania Hernandoz, Simon Burnett, Carolyn Buesi, Piers Dunn, Allyson Andrews, Mario Rodriguez, Judith Walsh.

# HYDE PARK CRESCENT NURSERY – MAY 1972

*Back Row:* Andrew Eden, Liza Joseph, Caspar Shand-Kydd.

*1st Row:* Steven Ritcheson, Rebecca Bunyan, Devang Jhaveri, Clarinda Weir, Amanda Foreman, Robert Harley, Fatima Al-Saleh, Jonathan Hynes.

*2nd Row:* Sabine Mruck, Piers Dunn, Lucy Wigram, Annabel Eker, Camilla Wigram, Giles Dunn, Sacha Llewellyn.

*3rd Row:* Nadia Ramoul, Adrian Donovan, Joanna Fraser, Phillip Apostolidis, Victoria Stratton, Emma Bourne, Philip Flaccomio, Katherine Kinross, Stephen Badger, Robert Beckman.

*4th Row:* Patrick Bourgeois, Fergus Gilroy, Stephanie Andrews, Jonathan Faiman, Laura Jane Antoniades, James Bethell, Sean Vaardal, Martin Birnhak, Wendy Kay, Andrew Lawson, Amanda Simpson, Nicolas Jackson, Hillary Wehrle, Mark Citron, Jane Biddle.

*Front Row:* Simon Cope-Thomson, James Datnow, Diane Goodman, Charles Kinross, Shireen Sagrani, William Bethell, Jonathan Kelly, Barbara Kopley, Simon Burnett, Karen O'Donohue, Max Hernandez, Kalina Ng, Daryl Lewis, Andrew Hynes.

recommended me Carol Cutner, whose daughter Louise by coincidence had been at the Hyde Park School.

To our delight his battalion is now stationed in Edinburgh and in the summer of 1992 he had had the great honour of commanding the Royal Guard at Balmoral, an exciting experience. Angus's two children are Thomas John Stewart Macpherson born in Inverness on June 19th 1988, and Lachlan James Stewart Macpherson, born in Gibraltar on September 24th 1990. To celebrate, at each christening a tree was planted at Balavil. The former is a tall willowy copper birch and the latter an oak.

The School at first we called Hyde Park Crescent Nursery – later to become Hyde Park School. The name Crescent was removed as it expanded to premises in other streets. Mr. Butler the head gardener of the Royal Parks drew to my attention that the name Nursery was used by the propagation beds in Hyde Park! Louise his daughter was at the School in 1982/83 and her mother, in spite of a busy medical career often walked back after school with Louise to Black Lion Lodge in Kensington Gardens. His advice on the colour schemes for the flower beds was invaluable.

The snags encountered at the Church Hall were not the decorators or the sanding of the floors, which were expensive, but the installation of the child size lavatories and basins as required by statutory law. The remaking of the cesspit and conduits, damaged by the 1939/45 German bombing was where the major problem lay. It was this which had caused the closing of the clinic and the doubtful survival of the Church.

I had made an appointment with the Bishop of London, the Rt. Rev. Gerald Ellison, a friend of the family. His wife later agreed to be a trustee when we formed the Hyde Park School Charitable Fund. I learned at first hand the problems to be tackled. The Bishop was unable to give any financial aid but his advice was invaluable. There was a community need and they felt that I was the person to fulfil it but did not think I could find the necessary funds. I asked the National Westminster Bank Manager for £10,000 but my capital was nil. I explained, with the staff being paid £5 per week and the fees £1.50 per child per week perhaps over a period of time I would be able to repay the debt. This was a huge challenge and the Bank Manager, Mr. Cartledge asked me to return later in the week with more detailed plans and costs. I brought with me a letter from the Bishop of London, and one from the Paddington Borough Council's Registrar stating that the premises would be suitable for children. The following week, my third visit, I took along Mr. Weinman, the builder to describe with great accuracy what the work involved would be. Cap in hand I stood before Mr. Cartledge. Several large companies with which my husband was associated banked in this branch, and after that meeting I became its debtor and he my advisor.

On receiving one large bill I telephoned urgently requesting the Bank Manager's advice. Blind with anxiety I could not remember his name and finally stumbled out "Mr Kneecap please". Shortly after came the reply "Kneecap here". This nickname was never to leave him. After many years of annual autumn meetings to finalize the accounts, he asked my husband and me to his farewell dinner. By this time he was at the Kingston-upon-Thames branch, and in front of a large gathering, I was asked to stand so all could see the originator of his nickname! He had been a loyal advisor from whom I had learned much, and I did enjoy that farewell feast.

I wrote to various charities and obtained around £500. The largest obstacle for the starting of the School was at least temporarily overcome.

The decorating finished and floors at the hall sanded, Nana and Mrs. Roney's nanny, Joyce Derrick, N.N.E.B., from Stirling, started on May 15th 1962 with Angus, Ishbel and Juliet Roney. Her mother Liz neé MacEwan and I were fellow Scots.

The Mitford children, Emma and Tessa are in the first school photograph. It was for me the beginning of a long and happy partnership with their mother, Lady Redesdale, and she became a Trustee of the School. Wilfred Hyde-White's children, Punch and Juliette, Anna Massey's son Simon Huggins, Julian Grosvenor and James Trumper were among the first pupils. Wilfred Hyde-White, a famous British Hollywood actor, was nearly seventy when his delightful children were born. When he was free, he personally walked them to school. Anna Massey came from the great acting family of that name. I remember seeing her in a play called "The Black Sheep of the Family" where the lead parts were played by her father, her mother and herself, which must be a West End record. Julian's family owns half of Belgravia, and James was the son of the head of Cluttons and Angus's closest friend.

In all twenty four children registered at that time. In September a huge step forward was achieved when we increased to thirty two with the inclusion of more children of friends and relatives. Andrew Macpherson, Anthony de la Rue, Amanda Cooper, Nicole Allen, and Jocelyn Tennant. Kate Loustau-LaLanne whose father was High Commissioner for the Seychelle Islands had in her class Helen Malcolm. Her father, Dougal, was in the Foreign Office as was Robert, now Lord Armstrong, whose step-daughter Polly McCowan was in the same group.

In the lower classroom, Sue Richards, then a N.N.E.B. student, had Edward Balfour, whose father is a distinguished officer in the Royal Greenjackets and his mother a Laing of Logie, the famous United Biscuits family, Thomas Norcliffe, the dentist's son, Daniel Weston whose father is a pop star, Angus Hilleary of the distinguished Isle of Skye family and Poppy Edwards. Her mother is on the Parish Council of St. John's and a great liaison officer for us.

The gardens along the south west side of the Church were sunny and sheltered. In half of the vaults we stored toys. In the rest the young Richard Branson started his first recording studio. It took a little time to agree when we would be silent enough for him and vice versa. He has made progress since that modest beginning and Virgin is now a household name.

The policy of the Church Commissioners came down in favour of revitalising St. John's Church and appointing a Vicar, the Reverend Cuthbert Scott, and it is now a thriving parish. The Church of St. John's started to be built in 1821 and was completed by Charles Fowler in 1832. My family thought if the Church was demolished not only would it be like losing an old friend but also a real feature of the architectural lay-out of the area. The preservation was achieved with help from Ivor Bulmer-Thomas of the "Friends of Friendless Churches Association". Vast repairs and improvements were required for the Church and the hall.

An early task for us was the building of a sand pit which was large and sited beside the children's main entry door. After an inspection we were told to change all the sand as local cats were using it as a lavatory. A metal cage, with a fine wire mesh and a stout padlock seemed to be the solution to this problem – it kept out both vandals and cats. This well guarded sandpit became the subject of an anonymous complaint which necessitated applying for planning permission!

The lease of the Church Hall expired in 1965 and we obtained a further extension. By then the Reverend Cuthbert Scott, ex Royal Navy, had become Vicar and embarked on a very ambitious improvement scheme which took two years to implement. The speeding up of the authorisation I'm sure was helped by our previous experience. Cuthbert Scott was innovative, intelligent and a pleasure to work with. This gave the School time to acquire a licence to continue the playgroup in the Mallinson's house at 1 Hyde Park Crescent and in the Palumbo's house a few doors along and to enlarge the number of children in Somers Crescent. A new roof-top sun room there enabled the numbers upstairs to expand to twenty four children, and with the departure of a now qualified Dr. Geoffrey Stanley-Jones to return to his beautiful West Country home, the basement was registered for a further twenty four. The re-building of Somers Crescent was nearing completion. Our rear garden lost its long arm into the mews, where another re-development had started eliminating the stables from which the actor Terry Thomas used to ride. No sooner had the writing paper been re-printed when our telephone number was changed from AMBassador 5077 to 262 8487.

We undertook to help to modernise the church hall, costing £70,000 to which the School contributed £10,000 and in return came a ten year lease at a moderate rate from September 1976. The musical and gifted Rev. Paul Rose had taken Cuthbert Scott's place. The hall was extended with new roof, new plumbing, and a new kitchen. One Nursery school father, the Persian Ambassador, whose daughter Eman had so enjoyed her time with us, aided the Church's appeal by a further £10,000. The result is the fine hall that stands today. New funds were raised by the parents holding coffee mornings etc., and a fund raising party for parents and friends arranged by the able and beautiful Diana Strathcarron – Andrew Macpherson's mother who tragically died shortly after from cancer.

Andrew Macpherson deserves a special mention. He was the second son of our cousin Diana Strathcarron, Ishbel's godmother, and was born in the same hospital, in the same month as Angus. Andrew's academic career could be described as undistinguished. He did however distinguish himself permanently in our history in another way. After losing his mother, he, his father and his nanny came to spend a Christmas holiday at Balavil with his huge, amiable and drooling bloodhound, Hoover, alleged to be the best behaved and most innocent dog in Britain. He left his mark! When they departed, the blue carpet had an enormous yellow puddle mark on it, and our pedigree black labrador bitch was pregnant!

When he and Angus left school at seventeen they put together a plan to drive all the way to Singapore and then go on to work for a spell in Australia. Angus's godfather, Prince Michel de Bourbon, who had spent an exciting part of the war closely with Tommy and is his oldest friend, gave the boys a third hand VW Camper van which had already been driven from Australia and therefore presumably knew the way back. Angus passed his driving test. Andrew failed, but obtained an International Driving Licence on the strength of his motorbike licence. They both went on a week's mechanics course, and in the end, not without adventure, they arrived at their destination. En route Andrew displayed perhaps for the first time his brilliant natural talent as a photographer. Thereafter he diligently developed that career and is today among the top two or three names in fashion photography in Europe and the U.S.A. with the professional name of Andy Mac.

Have you ever noticed how things happen in threes? In 1960 came Somers Crescent, Ishbel and Mrs. Ester Smith. Now she really was an asset to the establishment. The mother of five children, forty years old, skilled and punctual, you could time your watch as she came through the door. The first greeting was a detailed account of our misdemeanors, "You have dirtied the floor, that's no place for wet socks and who has been touching my Hoover". Ester remained until Somers Crescent was no longer ours and almost immediately ill health overcame her and her passing was my loss. She did all the washing and sewing for Hyde Park School until the new premises came into being. There was never any question of Kathy Stanley-Jones taking the towels to the Hall. Each one was hand embroidered with an emblem which could be identified by the child-user, either an elephant, lighthouse, or tree and so on. Ester maintained she needed to go across the road and see if the Lord was supervising the kitchen cleanliness in the Hall, as well as her soul. She had her statutory cup of tea there before returning to Somers Crescent. Kathy, a Staff Nurse at the School, and her medical student husband and child lived nearby in Norfolk Square. Her brother-in-law, Geoffrey lived in the basement of Somers Crescent until he qualified as a doctor and she visited him each morning.

Joyce, Kathy, Nana and I formed an excellent team. I interviewed the parents, collected the money and filled in the seemingly endless forms for our licences. The troublesome cesspit and conduit was much more important than I had realised and without its repair no licence would be granted. It involved lifting a large section of the south garden and on completion a long lawn and concrete pathway to the vestry door were made. The staff commented on the wet wait at the gate some days and we thought of several alternatives to alleviate the problem. A large umbrella or even a small portable tent, but a better answer emerged by chance. On an afternoon walk with the dogs, Angus and Ishbel, we spied a row of old redundant Buckingham Palace sentry boxes near the Knightsbridge army barracks on the south side of the park. The foreman laughed at me "only stuffy old generals want these as momentoes of their glorious years. What on earth do you want with one of these?" I explained. A big smile "Oh Guv wait till I tell 'em in the pub. For you two quid delivered free". It was a tremendous success, offering shelter and a landmark for new parents. Sadly its reign there was less than a decade. It became a shelter and focal point for the ladies of the night, then a distribution point for drugs. The Police found little packages secreted in the crevices and we found condoms scattered like confetti on the floor. In spite of real co-operation with the various organisations deeply involved in "Operation Sentry Box" it had to go. Up to Balavil, our Highland home on the A9 just south of Aviemore, and in the centre of Clan Macpherson country. To deliver this landmark to the prominent site it holds today cost an arm and a leg. The long cross bars of solid Victorian oak were not the easiest of things to transport, but it was worth it.

With every authority, Fire, Education, Health, and Safety Officers satisfied, the bills seem to mount inexorably so I, "Kneecap", Mr. Sherring, my husband and I had a meeting. The nursery school could only be viable with a minimum of seventy children. This number could carry a part time cleaner, part time laundress and a part time handyman as auxiliary staff. Staff wages were the main factor plus stationary, postage, printing and food. To reach this number required more than double the space the hall could supply. Plenty of parents offered me their qualified staff part-time as their young moved on to primary school. These girls had the opportunity of great luxury in Central London homes and work amongst the age group they enjoyed. Children too were moving into Somers Crescent and other newly completed houses. More and more I realised what a gift this backwater of peace was offering for town-bred children. A London evacuee in the Highlands in wartime had burst into tears on arrival as fear overcame her because there were no houses to keep the sky up! That poor lass genuinely believed that milk grew in bottles and chickens in cans.

In 1964 Angus left for St. Mary's Church of England Primary School, Bryanston Square and Ishbel and Tessa

Mitford a year later left us for the French Lycée. "You cannot expect our daughter to be rich or good-looking" Tommy said "but bi-lingual is a necessity". The crossroads had been reached, what route was the school now to take? It was immensely hard work, with dogs, lodgers, teaching, the Hyde Park School and the genuine desire to have seven children. I married a seventh child of the eldest of a large family of the Upper Spey Valley. Anything my mother-in-law could do, I could do also. But the big family was not to be mine, and abortive attempts had made my "get up and go" gone.

During our nomadic years we had spent Christmas regularly on the Isle of Arran. Tommy departed on Boxing Day, as at that time he had no time off between Christmas and New Year, but Nana and I remained with the "Yappers and Yellers", our dogs and children, as Lady Jean Fforde called them and her handsome son, Charles. I had marvellous Hogmanays visiting the cottages and taking a wee tipple in each. Finding a van in a ditch at Jean's gate, upside down, I insisted on getting out of our car to help. "I cannot think why you bother" she said "they are all drunk and will have tumbled onto the roof like leaves off a tree". How right she was. I cautiously approached through stinging nettles, in my evening dress and knocked on one of the windows, which was steamed up and opaque. Little activity ensued, then the clear West Highland voice of the cattleman emerged "No damage, no treatment, leave us to sleep". I did.

During this same period we spent our summers with Lady Macpherson at Speyville. Granny was a wise counsellor and kept her family in strict order of seniority when it came to bedrooms. On one occasion when I and the children had been relegated to the steading at the bottom of the garden, a miracle occurred, Captain Lindsay walked into my life. The steading had housed a horse and the groom and the carriage and the hay when the railway came to Newtonmore in the 1870's and brought prosperity to this outstandingly beautiful part of the country. Now more than a hundred years on, with no sanitation and little electricity in the steading, I greatly missed my husband to defend me, having been relegated there, after his two weeks holiday had finished. Ten years younger than my mother-in-law, who had been in her eighti-eth year when I married, Captain Lindsay entered Granny's living room. On seeing my tears he said nothing and walked through to where she was ironing the sheets. "I am finding Cluny Castle large and lonely this week, could you spare your youngest daughter-in-law and the children?" It brought great relief to overfilled Speyville and to Granny. A 1930 Rolls Royce drove up after lunch and took us to his home. Then started the first lesson in wisdom which was to prove such an enrichment to my life. "For dinner you will ask up your relatives". No, I pleaded, tomorrow perhaps but not now. He led me to the hall and the tall old fashioned telephone with the trumpet shaped earpiece. "Now, this evening for dinner, your mother-in-law will bless the occasion and the newly travelled will welcome not preparing a meal". I rang, they came. It was with great nervousness I met them. For fear I might tread on somebody's toes, I endeavoured to keep in the background. As we walked from the dining room after dinner to the drawing room, he took me aside into his study, "Jean, I always go to bed early but there are three members of the family to whom you have not yet spoken, please do that and I will go to bed". I did and he did.

My pupillage had begun and continued for many more holidays "every time with your hungry children" he said laughingly shortly before his death at ninety years of age, a month after my mother-in-law's funeral, she in her hundred and first year. These were great periods of recuperation and much of my future planning was done at Cluny Castle.

Angus and Ishbel left Hyde Park School for older academic centres. Malinee too had achieved her university goal in 1965. My sister's nanny, Marjorie Stevenson had joined the staff bringing Michael and Sheila Mallinson with her. Mrs. Doble, quiet, kind, understanding and thoughtful, spent the last three years of her young life with us, leukaemia rapidly taking her during one summer holiday.

Tommy and his T.A. soldiers marched through the Lairig Ghru from Braemar, where the Queen Mother, in her fishing waders stepped out of the River Dee to watch them go by. Rugby had given way to hockey, shooting and T.A.

camps. Nana on seeing Angus and Ishbel off to school had sensibly moved over to the Redesdale's where her primary love of babies were available in abundance. Nana's replacement came from beloved Speyside, Captain Lindsay's grandson had given us Marie-Noelle Fontaine with love. Love is the perfect description of her and she abounded in it. Her years as governess were very happy ones and her help with Ishbel and the French language were enormous. It is lovely now to hear of her and her happy marriage and family.

Dr. R.K.I. Kennedy helped greatly in my decision making. The sixth and last member of the family who founded Jenners, the Harrods of Edinburgh, he had entered our lives through Tommy and his continued interest in athletics. An Olympic High Jumper in Berlin in 1936, when I met him he was still much in demand as a track-side Doctor and a medical member of the Olympic and Commonwealth Games teams.

Here I must go back to the days of my engagement in the summer of 1953. Tommy and I met at the London Achilles Ball. He had arrived late at Gunters, then a popular ballroom in Curzon Street, with some friends after a London Scottish Rugby Club dinner, and danced the Highland Fling on my table. I remember one hairy knee and one shaved because of an injury that had had heavy sticky binding. He remembered my name and that I was completing my student year at a school starting with W. His unfortunate secretary wrote to all the schools starting with W in the Isis school book, to trace me so he could invite me to lunch. I received my invitation at Westonbirt and declined. Once my address had been identified the bombardment started. A tentative arrangement between a delightful architect and myself was quickly swept aside. The first outing together I fulfilled was a very happy London Scottish Club dance at Ripley. Next day we were to go to watch the Boat Race at Chiswick, then on to Richmond where the London Scottish were playing the famous Border club, Hawick. Tommy was at full back that day and I won no marks for describing him as a goalkeeper.

That was the day I was to meet him at Hyde Park Corner Underground, after he had done his Saturday morning office work. In my Morris Minor I hesitated on Hyde Park Corner, I thought I'd missed the turning, and reversed a little. After all there was hardly anyone about! In a trice a large policeman was tapping at my window "Where do you think you're going?" Rather tearfully I explained I seemed to have lost a boy I'd only just found. "Well, Miss, if you'll get off my foot I'll get in with you and we'll soon find him" and we did. Tommy was astounded to see a policeman alight from my car. Tommy and I met at the end of March, were engaged in May and married in September.

Meanwhile I had to complete my final qualifying term as a trainee teacher at Westonbirt School, Gloucestershire. When I got home to Alderley Edge at the end of July it all caught up with me and not even a Whitsun holiday in the south of France with the Trotter family put me right. My lungs, which so loathed Merseyside as a child, regained a high profile. Our three month engagement period found me in a nursing home, my hair shaved off with nervous eczema and my wheezes getting louder and louder. I really believed and still do, it was a brave man to take me on. "Your twin sister can attend the engagement party, arrange the bridesmaids dresses, and the reception and meet the relatives", the confident Tommy persisted. Anne must have done an excellent job, for I was still acceptable when four days before matrimony I emerged to depart for Edinburgh.

Much of my survival and self-confidence I attribute from then on to Dr. Kennedy. When attacks became acute he came in the night, long after most British doctors had given up home visits. On courses, holidays, and visits to his sons at Marlborough School, he left his telephone number.

The Nether Alderley Church, in which both my sisters were married, clearly could not be, in my eyes, the correct venue, seeing as how my circumstances had changed. "Do not worry about that" the engaging Tommy decreed, "your Aunts married in St. Cuthbert's Church of Scotland, Princes Street, Edinburgh, an ideal position for your family and mine", and that's what we did.

"A wife is awfully boring if she has no career", believed Tommy, and this principle was quickly put in hand. Visiting a friend at the Monkey Club in London's Pont Street a week after our honeymoon the formidable headmistress, Miss Joynson-Hicks passed by, tapped me on the head and said "How I wish people like you were on my staff". Being newly married I reported her words verbatim on Tommy's return from work. He telephoned the Head and the next day I started my career. Dr. Kennedy soon had much to resolve. Work even came before our Hyde Park Square flat and every major decision of mine seemed to require one or other of his medicaments.

When the School began to grow social life for the children became hectic. Julian Williams' father managed the Great Western Station Hotel at Paddington with the magnificent facility of space for parties, whilst Anthony de la Rue's father managed the Westbury Hotel, and Tara Shepard's father, Giles is Chairman of the Savoy Group. Jonathan Cape had access to printing wonderful coloured posters, and the parents of the Brim brothers and Stephen Duff-Godfrey of Laserbureau printed the invitations.

It was not long before the aged but ever alert Marguerite Vacani summoned me to tea at her famous dancing school. She recalled accurately coming to the Acton Reynold School, Shrewsbury when I was seventeen and presenting me with the dancing prize, and later teaching me to curtsey before being presented at Court on my marriage. "And now I hear you have a group of children and reading and writing has become your priority. Where is the band, the dancing and singing?" I tried in vain to explain the former and the latter existed but on dancing we were a little weak. Without further ado out came her diary, a visit on June lst, a written confirmation, and she started her classes in the Hyde Park School in September. She wrote that it coincided with the beginning of dancing lessons for Prince Andrew at Buckingham Palace. Her ear was always close to the ground, she gave her classes in every school of which she approved. Her personality enriched us, her musical gifts enhanced the life of every child that came into her care. "The Polka, even those with two left feet can manage the Polka" she would say.

The N.S.P.C.C. took Richard Branson's place when he left the church vaults and second hand clothing was sorted and periodic sales took place. I joined the Committee and the Paddington Branch raised many hundreds of thousands of pounds for children who needed protection. The Wigram sisters-in-law were the mainstays of the committee, with Mrs. Ruth Fitzgibbon. Sally Wigram's son, Max became an artist and twins Lucy and Camilla married a Sangster and a Cordle. Penny Wigram's Sophie is with the B.B.C. Lionel is in Los Angeles working in the world of films and Benjamin, the youngest, has made a mark with his love of photography. All six were at the Hyde Park School and contemporary with Ian Armstrong, the U.S. Economic Minister's son and Andrew Impey whose uncle we saw as an Eton house master. Lady Tavistock's eldest son Andrew Howland had a little fox, which wore a dog collar and happily walked along the street with Nanny to collect him. Clare Bardsley, Christopher Gregory, Kate Saunders, Nicholas Jones and Rima Te Wiata were others who joined that term. Rima's father Enia Te Wiata, a Maori, was one of New Zealand's greatest opera singers with a marvellous voice. He was also a fine traditional craftsman who personally sculptured the huge totem pole in New Zealand House in London's Haymarket from a tree shipped by my husband's company.

In the autumn term, Kate Saunders mother, Ann Saunders, who was secretary to Lord John North, became a helper in the school on his retirement. Soon after her arrival she became secretary, then administrative secretary and in 1988 the Principal. She has a great understanding for someone in unhappiness, as she herself lost her first husband through illness. Efficient, kind and competent, she deserved every step to the top.

Decisions, decisions were what I had to make in the 1960's. Would we close or go forward? I had time to think during a recuperative holiday with my American neighbour, Rita Beale to New England in the autumn of 1964. I returned to find the School's organisation had been trouble-free, and this gave me the realisation that it had a self-propelled future of its own. I would give up teaching and concentrate on giving to these youngsters a quality of life and teaching that would be second to none. I would seek and find new premises, and this I did.

Before I departed for Russia on a tour to advise on a school in Moscow, Lady Jean Rankin, whose three Asseily grandchildren had been in the school, offered me the opportunity to buy her house for the school. We had been offered 44 Albion Street on the retiral of the Rev. Scott, but were advised that it was not suitable.

With the American Embassy houses on each side of us, 35 Cambridge, her house, completed our quartet for the common garden. Mr. Jim Pettus at 6 Somers Crescent and Mr. T. Cowles of 12 Hyde Park Crescent, wrote and agreed it, the Gabbitas and Thring Feasability Trust recommended the £26,000 being asked for the lease. Chestertons, the Church Commissioners and the endless departments of Westminster City Council agreed and eventually I was there, mentally working out the colour schemes and collecting in the fees. There was an opponent – Tommy. His Highland instincts recoiled from the risk. Within a short period we had a change of American Embassy neighbours and the new ones disliked children's voices to such a degree that all the powers of the Embassy bore down upon Hyde Park School. Chestertons were obliged to help to find the School somewhere else to live. John Hollamby showed me every blade of grass in Connaught Village and explained which building could be given access onto it. Hastily and in desperation an offer for temporary use of 500 feet of garden at the rear of Connaught Street was made. The quest for expansion had been solved and its creation into premises suitable for children, satisfactory to bureaucracy and rewarding and creative for me, made exciting times ahead.

# CHAPTER THREE

During the years as Principal of the School my Christian faith and the fellowship of the Community played a prominent part. One of the conditions of employment for staff was that they were of the Christian faith, of any denomination. All staff were professionals and we had few problems. We would set aside a number of hours each week with all the employees, to sort out any grievances, real or imaginary. Most of the discussions were about timetables or meal time coverage. Perhaps lessons could be learned by much larger companies from this. If one half knows what the other half was doing, there would be less strife at work.

One of the greatest services of the Hyde Park School was its care of children in emergencies. This service was available fifty two weeks of the year, including Bank Holidays. It enabled families who needed sudden short stay care the opportunity to bring their children, confident that they were safe and happy.

Play comes naturally to every child, it relaxes and relieves the tensions which can arise, especially for the modern city-dweller. It should have a prominent part in children's every day life. In the Emergency Service, in modern terminology Extended Day Care, the groups were small. A newcomer could participate in whatever activity was taking place. It proved extremely useful for the children of diplomats, whose parents might suddenly arrive in Britain and had made no prior booking for the children. The service provided by the Hyde Park School was clearly meeting a real need. Outside the School one could hardly move for cars with bodyguards and nannies. Children were recommended to the School by the Hon. Diana Makgill, C.V.O., of the Foreign Office Protocol Department. One placement in ten came from her. Diplomats' children were not always Christians. We had regularly children of the Jewish, Muslim and Hindu

Faiths. When parents placed their children at the School it was made absolutely clear that we practised Christian values and fellowship, and very very few objected.

St. Mary's Hospital being so near filled many of the emergency places. The non-sick child of a family was sent to us and frequently it was later joined by the invalid in convalescence.

When we first started, these facilities only allowed house-trained two year olds as our youngest entrants but later there were so many requests from parents that admission started at one year old. A well equipped crèche was started in the able and qualified care of Susan Richards. She had spent her post school year at Hyde Park School as a YOP student. Then after obtaining her N.N.E.B., she returned as a nursery nurse, and latterly she took charge of the baby group.

One of the highlights of the School calendar was the Nativity Play. We chose children from the older groups to take part, and they enthusiastically learned Christmas Carols such as "Away in a Manger", and "Once in Royal David's city". Kay Munro threw her heart and soul into achieving a very high standard. On the great day either a halo slipped or a shepherd lost a head-dress, but the play always reached the end, and they marched off down the aisle in two's with many a wet eye in the congregation of parents and friends.

The priority for children's entry to the School in the early days went to my relations, personal friends and those with whom I had a long association. From the community came the printer's, the estate agent's, the florist's, the fishmonger's, the baker's and the vet's children and what fun they were. One morning an excited boy arrived and said, "My daddy has a new car". "So has mine and it has four doors" was his friend's quick and inaccurate reply. "My daddy's car has got five doors". "My daddy has a submarine in the Serpentine with a blue front door". That silenced all!

A school's needs are varied and I required help from many. Ivor W. Rowell, Builders, of 4 Junction Place put up the large oak wooden gates to the south entrance to the Church Gardens. With my husband's work in Mallinson, the Timber Merchants, I had the opportunity to buy magnificent mellow oak which lasted for thirty years and when the Trust sold the school still looked as if they would last at least another century. Mr. Weinman of Kininmonts, Builders, and Mr. Davis of Pyrene, the Fire Protection Engineers, organised the alterations to the hall including new children's lavatories, the roof extension at 4 Somers Crescent and many smaller requirements too. The floor covering was laid in the hall and staircase by Mr. Page of 3 Ingersoll Road. He spent days hidden from daylight scraping and tidying underground vaults and putting up hooks and shelving there. Miss Gibb made the curtains, and the staff uniforms were cared for by Chiswick Laundry who delivered weekly. Mr. McQueen of 34 Bathhurst Mews mowed the lawn and I think we must have kept Fowles Ltd., the Lawn Mower Engineer and Cutler of 22 Bell Street in business looking now at the many receipts. James Matt Ltd., General Ironmongers of 166 Star Street was where Jim Hale our handyman called in with "my friend", the name given to a variety of fellow workers at Selfridges of Oxford Street. They came by in the evenings for a mug of hot tea and cleaned, put up hooks, moved equipment or resolved any other needs of the day, and on summer Sundays carried my husband off for the occasional game of rural cricket.

New deliveries of toys came regularly from Hamleys in Regent Street, Abbots and Galts. From Elswick-Hopper, in Barton-on-Humber, came the strongest of tricycles of every size. The wear and tear was great and they and the dolls prams would be taken up every holiday to 194 Edgware Road to the Arcadia Pram Repair Service. The dolls were often donated. Nana's aunt, Miss Parker would knit the most beautiful clothes including bonnets, mitts, bootees and knickers. The dresses she made were all easy to fasten and wash. Nana's father made wooden toy railway engines with carriages, which were very popular. We needed Albion Electrical at 24 Albion Street almost as frequently as United Dairies' daily deliveries of milk. The Church Hall lights seemed to have switches or bulbs in awkward places, requiring frequent attention. I have a feeling they found the staff pretty too!

Speed Decor at 47 Kendal Street, painted and re-painted tricycles, benches and nursery tables. Coloured sticky paper and big black scrap books came from either S.R. Hodges of 42 Connaught Street or Sheldon Stationers of 12 Porchester Place, one for each little person to fill with numbers and letters and pictures. The last payment before decimalisation in 1971 was to the Isaac brothers, owners of Hogg the Chemist. Each member of staff had a first aid kit equipped exactly as specified by the Health and Safety Officer, a regular visitor, who changed the rules and require-ments with great frequency, which the Chemist patiently and perfectly supplied, always stocking our needs as they moved from one shop to another in Connaught Street at apparently Chesterton's whim.

The Lawsons held a particular place in our life for we kept Shetland sheep dogs. To Londoners, vets are very needed people. Injections against lamp post disease, or diarrhoea, problems of diet and exercise all be-come disproportionately big in a city environment. Poop-a-scoops came in and caused the unfortunate animals even more canine anxieties. Our sheep dogs firstly were called Rhuara and Misty. Then came Sheena and Morag who gave us a puppy – a sort of biology lesson for Angus and Ishbel, Shoona and Pattack, who also gave us a puppy, a biology lesson for Duncan a decade later. Not all went smoothly. Sixty three days after Duncan had taken her to a sire she went into a coma, instead of labour. Our beloved Margaret greeted me with great anxiety. We rang the surgery and although only a street away Margaret's legs could not manage the distance. We drove there, I carried the dog in and rushed out to park the car. In two brief minutes it had been stolen or towed away. Once home we reported it but the Police and the parking pound found nothing. Months later, after regular contact with the police station, they suddenly discovered it had been in a police pound all the time. The car came back, and my husband insisted on substantial compensation for the expenses we had had without the car. He got it, and my regard for both him and the police went up!

Duncan walked in carrying a large male pup, destined to be twice his mother's size and amazingly like Margaret's dog Nicholas, not the chosen sire. "You didn't tell me Mother – babies are born between the spare rib and backbone" said Duncan. A Caesarian had been necessary. To prevent feeding problems the wise Mr. Lawson had chosen that place!! One of the many passing taxis collected Pattack and Margaret and the latter spoiled the former totally and never once was there a complaint about puddles or messes. Shamus the puppy joined our household with his aunt and mother and two black labrador bitches at Balavil. As I write he still rules the household. Kay Munro's tortoise lasted twenty five years but ended his days at the vet because he woke from hibernation, fell over and was damaged by pigeons! Michael Lawson gave to all comers clear loud instructions in his resonant North Country voice, which could be heard the length of Connaught Street, always firm and usually right. His charming ballet dancer wife gave him three sons: Timothy married a Dane, lives in Copenhagen and is senior partner of Price Waterhouse there; Andrew and Nicholas are doctors. Nicholas the youngest won our only musical scholarship. At five years of age he had perfect pitch.

Miss Child and Miss Humphries, Co-Principals of the Montessori College at 22 Princes Gate, the only British College started by the great Madam Montessori, in which my aunt Miss Wilson took a great interest from its start in the 1930's, came to visit us. They were having management problems and made approaches to see if I would join them. The Montessori method of teaching allows each child to progress at his or her own pace, if travel or ill health has left a gap in basic knowledge which on a one to one basis can be filled. It is not always the answer for the intellectual or for children who need the stimulus of group activity. I felt it was too great a commitment for the moment and declined.

From this College came Alice Greenwell. She started the first Montessori group in the Long Garden, in the upper Classroom in 1969. A quiet disciplinarian, who used the system sensibly so that even the lazy could not pretend it was a day of play only. Her care of the equipment, with which she worked for over ten years before her marriage, and for several years after she was Mrs. Walker, was perfect. Later she was joined by Cary Cornwallis, daughter of Lord Cornwallis, a friend of ours.

In 1978 we had the special addition of Elizabeth Lady Colville of Culross. Following a car accident in which she and her four sons were injured, some three years earlier, Elizabeth Colville trained at St. Nicholas Montessori College and joined the staff in the Hall. Her sons, Charles, James, Fergus and Geordie were the greatest help, and with practical hands laid turf, built decorative walls, paved playgrounds and decorated classrooms. It was a productive time for us all and their help removed many of the trials of new buildings. She left us in 1981 to take on a small school in Kensington. As a training ground for starting one's own group, Hyde Park School excelled and over the years many did so. I have visited several, and heard of several others. It gives me great pride to think that all over Britain the much needed Extended Day Care has proved itself, with success wherever a centre has been started. Philippa Summerskill was one of these. Like her mother, Edith she kept the Summerskill name from her grandfather. Her father was the Westminster Coroner, and his other daughter Yvette Crompton was at the School.

We were offered staff from so many sources that I was spoilt for choice with marvellous people like Debbie Sanders who came from Cambridge, a much loved and natural teacher, Dawn Tritton and Beth Wareham, the practical and kind Mrs. Molly Piper and Carol Taylor, who returned after a three year absence training as a primary teacher to work with the five to six year olds in the newly completed classroom. That year too, in 1984, Theresa Roche, both nursery and Montessori trained, came and was one of the fortunate few to find a flat, at 98 Bell Street, which she could afford. Accommodation was always at a premium in Central London. Judith Somervell shared what had been our flat in 16 Hyde Park Square in 1982, after completing her training at the Chiltern Nursery Training College in Reading and joining the staff. From Chiltern too came Caroline Barlow, Drew Conroy's nanny, and Ann Chatley, Sheila Mallinson's nanny.

Una Farrell and Margaret Langley were both long established nannies with the Strathcarrons and with Lord John Cholmondeley and their help and guidance was much appreciated by the less experienced youngsters.

One of the more boring chores that happens in Nursery Schools is the term by term stock-taking of equipment. We divided it into three sections. The items were all washed and then returned or repaired, or replaced. Each member of staff with a group would submit a list of all her needs. For example the New Hall used thirty three yellow mugs, one mop, a dust pan and brush. Also recorded were the sixteen tables, thirty eight chairs, one Red Cross box, four shoe lockers, three waste paper baskets, four dolls prams, six push chairs, duvets, eiderdowns, pillows, mobile beds, record players, records, books of childrens songs, tapes. We listed books such as The Elephant, Teddy, 101 Dalmatians, Victories A.B.C., Little Boy Blue and Sailing Boats. These were all checked and where practicable repaired.

The selection of workers for the nursery was of vital importance. They were all Nursery Nurses Education Board Certificated or of similar qualification. In the 1980's there started to arrive from several London Borough Councils well qualified students with certificates in Child Care and Child Welfare. We recruited wherever practical from the Scottish Colleges of Edinburgh, Glasgow, Aberdeen and Dundee which had excellent courses. Marjorie Stevenson from Glasgow who was Michael Mallinson's nanny, Julia Thain from Edinburgh, Marion Hall from Aberdeen who looked after Duncan and Kate Campbell who looked after the next generation Michael Mallinson's daughter Rosanna. Michael, a Cambridge architect and winner of one of London's Docklands Design Awards, helped us greatly to overcome drain design queries on which the Inspector, Mr. Salomen, needed clarification and innumerable drawings, when Linwood the Essex-based builders were finalising the School buildings in the Long Garden later on.

As the next term got under way in 1969, following a miscarriage, I went off to Monte Carlo with Lady Jean Fforde to her cousins Prince Rainier and Princess Grace of

Monaco. The fertility pills I had been taking had given me a multiple conception so I remained pregnant. When Duncan was born on December 28th, Princess Grace said I must have had an affair with a beach boy and we called the baby Monaco Macpherson for many months. She became an extra god-mother to him.

From August 19th to September 6th of the following year I was in Russia with Rita Beale and we came back via Helsinki. The Russian trip arose from the School. Rita's husband was American Economics Minister in London and had been in Russia. He learned that the Western Embassies there were keen to set up kindergarten facilities, and they wanted an expert to come over and give them the "know-how". The invitation came to me, and Rita as a fluent Russian speaker was a marvellous chaperone. When we arrived in Moscow, we found the Russians had heard about us too, and also wanted my "know-how", so I found myself with a trip to Kiev and to Sochi on the Black Sea, complete with a very nice Russian driver and the compulsory in-terpreter. In a restaurant in Kiev, where there was music, I was amazed when a well-dressed young Russian came to our table, bowed formally, and in good but stilted English re-quested of the formidable six foot tall Rita, that he could be permitted to dance with her daughter!

We went by hydrofoil down the great waters of the Volga, and were given the main deck cabin. The deck was crowded with mainly large females. Suddenly Rita said "Now we'll show them the infrastructure of the U.S.A." From her suitcase she took out elasticated undergarments of every style and dimension, and got me to hang them very visibly in the cabin. Next she opened the window, and called out in Russian "Ladies, if you can get into them, you can have them". In a moment the cabin was a mass of bodies, skirt-less and in large identical blue bloomers, enthusiastically wiggling their way into these exotic garments. Minutes later the cabin was empty and not a trace of undergarments remained.

We were taken on an excursion to a Georgian vineyard. I liked one white wine very much, and mindful of my husband's love of good wine I asked if I could buy some. The manager gallantly gave me a case, and said he would send it to London. I was doubtful of the practicality of his offer and was astounded when it arrived, nearly a year later. It was delicious.

There was an odd epilogue to this trip. Rita had asked the interpreter to call if she was ever in London. We all do this when we are abroad. One day out of the blue she had a phone call that Valentina was in London looking after a trade delegation, and could she come to tea in a couple of day's time. Rita told her husband in the U.S. Embassy and all sorts of alarm bells rang. In those ultra-cold war days such contacts were considered so unusual that they meant spying, defection, kidnaps, or some sort of skull-duggery. The Beales' house and ours were visited by the "Spooks". Recording equipment went under the tea table, and on the chosen afternoon two large C.I.A. men lay under Rita's bed on the floor above, watching and listening with probes through the ceiling to the drawing room below. M.I.5 were also in on the act, but unfortunately came on the wrong day and Tommy had to check up with ex-army friends in intelligence that they were in fact genuine! As it happened the C.I.A. recording machine failed to work, and Valentina ate cucumber sandwiches and simply made normal ladies' tea-time conversation.

In the spring Ann Saunders came to work for us permanently. She is now the Principal of Ravenstone House. She first brought her daughter Kate to the school in April. In the autumn Mrs. David Donne brought Edward and at the same time Clare Bardsley, Andrew Impey and William Rollason joined.

The following are extracts from a letter I received from Kay Munro:

"I joined the nursery school in January 1965. My youngest son Stewart had started at Connaught House. You, Jean were abroad on your slow sugar boat trip to Jamaica, when you had a patch on your lung and were to be away for some nine weeks. I had known your husband, Tommy, before you. He and my husband, Allan, played rugby together at the London Scottish. You asked if I would come in and look after the old hall, this was before its up-date, with Joan Marsh. Kathy Stanley-Jones, student then doctor's wife from 47 Norfolk Square, and the lovely Jan McSwinney, daughter of Judy and Pat, who was a Housemaster at Harrow, were the other members of the staff at the time. I found the first few weeks dealing with twenty four children aged between three and four totally exhausting and very noisy. However I did get used to it and when you came back I agreed to stay on and I did for twenty five years.

Jane MacDonald of Clanranald, wife of the Clan Chief joined the staff and brought her two sons, Angus and Andrew. Wendy Boissier joined the Montessori team. Her father's teaching gifts as housemaster at Sherborne school shone through. We were all sad when matrimony stole her from us, and she became Mrs. Malcolm McVittie. She now lives in Helensburgh and has a family of her own. We benefited in those days from employing several N.N.E.B.'s from relatives and parents. Local nannies like Joanne Crossley from Mrs. George Martin at 5 Somers Crescent, who brought along their charges with them and worked in the morning. We had several happy parent/staff arrangements. I remember two Scottish nannies who came down, Marion Hall to look after Duncan and Gillian Mackintosh, Douglas and Ann's daughter from Newtonmore, to work in the nursery. Marjorie Stevenson from the Glasgow College who came in 1964 and Edith Maton in 1969 come to my mind in this category. They worked in your sister's house. Caroline Taylor, who was with Tessa Kennedy in Hyde Park Gardens with Milicia and Dillon Kastner was another marvellous girl who worked with me in the Long Garden and Hall between 1977 and 1982. The arrangement suited us all extremely well. When St. John's was being altered we all went to the Long Garden. We were over there for two terms. Although slightly cramped we had a lovely summer and having the use of the garden was a real bonus. Princess Helen of Romania came as an extra pair of hands and greatly enjoyed the experience.

It was when we returned to the hall that we were asked for £10,000 and given a ten year lease. The hall did look lovely especially the new loo's and the kitchen. The disappointment was that the large dividing doors that had partitioned off the hall into two classrooms had been removed. There was a large reduction in the storage area we had for our chairs, toys and valuables. The old tower which we used had become the Vicar's exclusive area. The entrance had been changed from the south side of the building to the north. We came in through a new corridor and then into the big hall, but we still had doors leading out into the garden. We continued to use the vaults downstairs as our storage space for the toys. After negotiations long and hard we managed to obtain the basic requirements needed for children's welfare and safety."

Alice Colman, from the famous mustard family, Montessori trained, worked on and off with Kay Munro for five years, standing in for her holiday periods. A very warm personality, with a great love of horses. She made us laugh with her tales of equine adventures. We had the Aga Khan's niece, the Begum Pasha Houran come to the school as an Embassy placement. Seven Ambassadors' children, one child to each group, came into the school at any one time. They generally had the luxury of English speaking nannies and often had a good command of the English language before they came into the school and their parents posting allowed them to remain twelve months. Alexander Galitzine, the Lutyens children, Guy Hollamby, whose father was the Senior Partner with Chestertons, Timothy Boyd, John de Lisle and the Young-Taylor boys also joined the school at that time.

We had American Embassy neighbours on each side of us in Somers Crescent – the Beales and the Petersons. The latter were in the Special Services and those that followed him were also in the F.B.I. or C.I.A. We had many successive good and delightful neighbours and were very glad that the Embassy owned these properties. We also shared our garden with Number 35 Cambridge Square. It was Lady Jean Rankin, a lady-in-waiting to the Queen Mother and native of the Isle of Mull who stayed there. This completed our quartet. By then three of her grandchildren were at the school.

The psychiatrist from St. Mary's Hospital sent his daughter Philomena Keet, the Tavistocks sent their second child Robin Russell, Damian Rayne, Lord Rayne's son, came from Holland Park, Charles Fellows from Gloucester Square and Edward Saatchi whose father's publicity did so much for Prime Minister Thatcher, joined in the same term. The Gordon Deans were something special, mother and father each with a child on the back of their bicycle, flowing hair, flowing gown and bubbling with enthusiasm. Petronella moved on to great heights as I am sure her brother did too – but I shall remember him exultant at mastering how the grandfather clock worked!! In his pursuit of knowledge he had clambered inside and totally destroyed the valuable irreplaceable family heirloom.

Mrs. Newley, the actress Joan Collins and wife of Anthony Newley, the actor and producer, had her two children Tara and Sasha at the School. Tommy and I at that time had to go to Malta as he had business in the dockyards. Whilst we were there, they were making a film. Anthony Newley kindly invited us to visit the open air set and lunch with the cast. We were fetched from our hotel, the Phoenicia, in a vast old Rolls Royce, probably the only one on the island, and were driven along bumpy side roads to a remote and beautiful sandy beach. I remember the scene vividly, vast numbers of people were milling around with their equipment, in what seemed to the uninitiated to be total chaos. The sequence being shot in the brilliant sunshine was a dream fantasy, and, as we arrived, fifty naked blonde ladies emerged from the surf to run across the sand and leap into a huge bed with the star.

Time and again the Director, not satisfied, called for a repeat, until at last they had to stop for lunch as the girls were all covered with goose pimples. At the break, amid the general confusion, we were most impressed with the professionalism of the dragon-like continuity ladies who photographed every performer so that at the restart, they would have each bead of sweat or dirt or crease in precisely the same spot. It was a fascinating and memorable day and the Newleys were excellent hosts.

On my return I started looking for permanent country premises, thinking a country base nearer than Inverness-shire might be practical. Hyland Hall in Essex was the only scheme I seriously considered outside of London, but it had no appeal for Tommy "why be practical when Badenoch is so beautiful?"

Angus almost had the opportunity of acquiring a croft called Upper Knock of Clune above the village of Newtonmore. When Angus Stewart died we understood he had left it to him. He too had a sister called Ishbel and he was an earlier generation cousin of the family through my husband's grandmother. Sandy, the brother of Angus Stewart who had children contested this bequest. We therefore, after one summer holiday there, thought it would be better not to make this our family home and did not pursue the matter.

Angus and Ishbel attended the school in Newtonmore in August as they did not re-start at Hill House and the Lycée until the end of September – holidays so long as to be almost boring. Ishbel had been born on July 16th 1960, late in the evening and a couple of days earlier than expected. I had been required to go into Westminster Hospital in advance. Tommy was dining in Bayswater with our good friends, Sir John Wood, a High Court Judge, and his lovely wife Anne, with whom we had a memorable holiday sailing in the Mediterranean. The phone rang as they were having a second leisurely cup of coffee. "This is the Westminster Hospital, your wife has just delivered you a son". He rushed to the hospital and reached the maternity ward just in time to see a bright red and clearly female baby, covered with black hair, being carried out of the labour room for cleaning up. He had great difficulty in believing this was his, but as she grew the likeness and temperament were unmistakeable. The black hair is now long and blonde and curly. Like her father she is a workaholic, and by sheer ability and effort became the first woman director of Barclay de Zoete Wedd Corporate Finance, leading her own team of men. She lives independently in another freehold mews house two doors away from us.

She started at Hyde Park School, then entered the French Lycée. Her ear for music and languages was strong and her father was very enthusiastic that she should be bi-lingual. He admired the French educational system, although he did not have the courage to put his sons outside the conventional frame! I remember an amusing incident during Ishbel's early years at the Lycée. At five years of age she collected a half-penny from a group of her classmates, walked out of the playground illegally, bought Smarties against school rules and then distributed them amongst her friends. I was called the next day and carpeted for her enterprise.

Angus, Ishbel and I stood in The Mall, with thousands of others, on January 28th 1965 to watch the funeral procession of Sir Winston Churchill, while their father was in the Abbey. We failed to see the union-jack draped guncarriage pass, as at the vital moment a police horse in front of us performed copiously a natural function. Ishbel turned enthusiastically to me saying "my horse does that, I like the smell". In later years she became a most accomplished rider, winning innumerable rosettes at junior and intermediate level. We were very proud of her, but it meant that I became an equine taxi driver taking our hideously unmanoeuvreable horse box all over Scotland!

It was entirely due to a skiing accident in the Cairngorms that she left the Lycée, where she had gone with her friend Tessa Mitford, one of the family who come up repeatedly in my story. Tessa's elder sister, Emma, continued in the French system. Ishbel's cartilage was badly damaged and it involved a large plaster cast. There were one thousand pupils at the Lycée and two hundred in her year (five teachers and forty pupils per class). They shut the doors three minutes after the beginning of each class and she could not get up the five floors to her classroom in time. She was not permitted the luxury of using the staff lift and so it became necessary for her to do most of her work at home. I used to call each day to collect it, she would spend about half an hour there once a week seeing the relevant teachers. When the end of the year came, her exam results were good but because of her very poor attendance record, she was asked to repeat her year which was unacceptable. With her good grades she was recommended to one of the most academic British boarding schools for girls, Wycombe Abbey. Ishbel passed her entrance exam. She and her friend Caroline Aldred needed to have extra tuition in Latin and English history as they were not on her Lycée curriculum and this was rectified by attending Miss Hugh Jones Tutors where they both had an adventurous time.

We bought for Ishbel a horrible little white pony called Chloe who broke Tessa Mitford's arm, tossing her onto the gate. She was the first animal we had at Balavil and had every possible vice. Having mastered her, Ishbel could master any horse.

Miss Fisher, the Archbishop of Canterbury's sister, was her headmistress at Wycombe and perhaps to defy her discipline Ishbel took up smoking behind the school lavatories and became a firm packet-a-day smoker. Being an asthmatic myself I find it very sad to see her ruining an excellent pair of lungs. Because we all eat porridge, she will not touch it, and I think because we do not smoke she has to. She was born a lovable and sometimes infuriating rebel and a creative individual thinker. After her 'O' level exams she made a pronouncement that she would leave the school. We endeavoured to persuade her to remain, I can't think why as it nearly killed us and did not work. Father decreed that there would be no schooling in London for Madam under any circumstances and so we looked elsewhere for an alternative. Girls were just starting to come into Fettes College in Edinburgh. It was central, it was on our way up to Balavil and it was in the family tradition. Mr. Chenevix Trench was the Headmaster. Whilst he was at Eton we had met him. My husband promised me faithfully that he would come to the Fettes interview.

The night before the great meeting, Ishbel, my husband and I spent at the North British Hotel, in 1985 it sadly for us became the Balmoral from which we had been married and with which we had a close and happy association. We had a dinner the night before, entertaining amongst others Prince Rainier and Princess Grace of Monaco, and when I awoke the next morning I found pinned to the pillow the following message "Left you the chauffeur, left you the car, cannot make the meeting, hope it goes well". With a broken ankle in plaster, we set off to Fettes College. We were delegated a young gentleman to show us around the school. We went up and down innumerable flights and I am certain we visited every tower and turret. The headmaster and his wife greeted us warmly. He looked at me and I at him and we both knew of the circumstances of our previous meeting. I had removed my elder son not once from his care but twice. He could not have been kinder, he could not have been more considerate, he could not have been more embarrassed and his wife kept us going. She was strong, charming, amusing and supportive.

We got through that ghastly interview and Ishbel was placed in the school but living in digs outside as was then the pattern.

Ishbel was determined that Italian was going to be her second language and Fettes promised to arrange tuition outside the normal curriculum, but it never materialised. She had an eventful career at Fettes with most satisfying final academic results. In her last year she was made Head Girl for the girls in the school. This luxury lasted for six hours. She rang me in the evening to tell us. What she did not tell me was that one of her many escapades had caught up with her and the headmaster, even though he was a great fan of Ishbel's, had to take notice.

After Fettes, and turning down a Cambridge opportunity, she chose to go to Edinburgh University where at last she could do Italian along with her French. It was a happy four years, after a grotty start with a hostel room-mate on the Royal Mile, who insisted on bringing a young man home at night. The four year course allowed her to have six months in Florence, where she joined the Cathedral Choir and had the marvellous experience of touring Italy with them, and the less attractive experience of having her bottom pinched black and blue by passing Italian males. It also included a year in France, at the Sorbonne, whose course demands were limited and left her lots of time to learn perfect French in the social round. After a term staying with a family in Paris, she had the good fortune to be lent a cottage in the grounds of her brother's godfather, Prince Michel de Bourbon Parme's home at Versailles. His family, and particularly the twins, Michel and Dimitri of Yugoslavia, helped to make this a very happy year.

After taking her degree, it was Ishbel's turn to travel far afield and she went off to Zimbabwe, with her close friend Eleanor Fraser from Moniack near our Scottish home. Elie is as tall as Ishbel and has beautiful long red-gold hair, so she and Ishbel must have made a striking pair in Zimbabwe, where the Fraser family have a farm. Then it was London, and time to find a job. Ishbel's urge was for industry, but it was hard to pinpoint the right opening, so she turned to merchant banking and has never looked back. She showed her father all the offers, and he suggested Barclays Merchant Bank, as it then was, as their two year training course had a good reputation. Barclays selected her, I know not on what grounds, and their judgement has proved absolutely right. She loves what she does and all the City talk is that she does it extremely well, with flair, great diligence and attention to detail. Long hours are involved, early and late, but what a joy to see such a happy and successful and beautiful person.

My philosophy in the School that all children of all origins mix happily together was clearly working. They all need a stable, orderly, and safe community life and a clear grounding in letters and numbers before their formal schooling starts.

Emily Sassoon, Alexander and Morgan Watts, Jonathan Foreman, Dominic Gibbs, Alexander Konialidis, Lesley Gore were all at this time new arrivals at the School. Clarinda Weir, sister of Lord Inverforth, also came to the School as did my godson Rupert Mitford who was born on July 18th 1966. Robert Harley came that term. I met his mother again at a railway station years later rushing to catch the train to Oxford. The other lady with her told me that his Oxford College had just phoned to say that Robert had taken his own life. How fortunate most of us are, to be spared such tragedies.

The younger daughter of Lord Swansea, Louisa Vivian, joined us, and on the sad loss of her mother, her sister Amanda and brother Richard spent their "A" level year of study living with us at 4 Somers Crescent. Nanny Sassoon also came into our lives. She was a member of one of the families who encouraged me and finally persuaded me to make the move to larger premises.

January was a very interesting month. We started with Mrs. Shand-Kydd's arriving at the school with her son Casper. Casper later went with Duncan to Eton and we followed his progress very closely. He had developed leukaemia as a child and we kept him six months longer than we would normally have done because of this. Kay Munro had to take a month off as she had fallen and broken her ribs, and

Esther had her daughter killed in a car crash the same week. You would say these excitements, successes, sorrows and tragedies are the very substance of life in the sort of active community we had created.

A fellow elder in St. Columba's Church Christopher Strang sent to us in Somers Crescent Melville Matheson as a lonely and homeless Scot, and we had him with us for many months. He was a skilled opthalmological technician in the famous Moorfields Eye Hospital, a quiet, unassuming man whose hobby was organising the Church's tennis club. Suddenly he started to get headaches whose severity I found worrying. One day they were so bad he could hardly bear it, and I decided to send for an ambulance to take him to hospital, feeling he would get more medical attention in that way than he had so far received on previous visits. As it happened, he did – he was seen by chance by a very well-known neurologist, who sent him packing with an aspirin or two and told him to come back in a fortnight. I met him walking, or rather stumbling home. I was horrified, took him straight to the Glasgow train and telephoned his mother, He was in a bad state on arrival, was admitted to Glasgow Southern Infirmary and operated on that night for a serious brain tumour. His life was saved, and all his faculties, and he is now happily back at work. He returned to Somers Crescent until it was sold and was a great addition to the household.

The fascinating mixture of parents was one of my great pleasures. I recall the three Sieff boys, Patrick, Simon and David, all bright as buttons. The Sieffs introduced me to the world of Jewish charities, and they really do look after their own in need with true family spirit. Then there was David MacDuff and Alexandra Carnegie, children of the Duke of Fife, and from a contrasting milieu Nabila Khashoggi. Our neighbour Lady Jean Rankin's Asseily grand-children were always consumed with anxiety about their Lebanese home. The Queen Mother used to visit Lady Jean, and the children and I occasionally met her in the street as she came or went. We have the pleasure of being slightly known to her as my husband commanded the London Scottish (T.A.) of which she is the Honorary Colonel. She often has recalled how when

## HYDE PARK NURSERY SCHOOL – 1973

*Back Row:* Nicholas Lawson, Amanda Foreman, James Bethell.

*1st Row:* Jonathan Hynes, Emma Hyman, Robert Beckman, Simone Wakewella, Carlos Dominguez, Teddy Kessler, Katherine Kinross, Simon Woodman.

*2nd Row:* Devang Jhavieri, Wendy Kay, Radi Nabulsi, Fergus Gilroy, Jane Biddle, Sean Vaardal, Ana-Maria Lockton.

*3rd Row:* Rebecca Copeland, Phillip Flaccomio, Nardia Dei, Ingrid Ijsselstein, Duncan Macpherson, Tara Shephard, Jonathan Kelly, Laura-Jane Antoniades, Jimmy Lengemann, Charles Kinross.

*4th Row:* Max Hernandez, Simon Wicks, Hilary Wehrle, Benjamin Leon, Kate Joseph, Simon Cope-Thompson, William Bethell, James Hyman, Jason Simpson, Amanda Simpson, Daniel Kelly, Melissa Thompson, Patrick Bourgeois, Daniel Gold.

*Front Row:* James Strauss, Jason Eker, Emily Johnson, Diane Goodman, Daryl Lewis, Alexander Lee, Natalie Papageorgio, Charles Bryant, Cathy Ijsselstein, Dillon Kennedy, Alexander Beeber, Vimi Shan, Nicolas Beitner, Andrew Hynes.

**HYDE PARK NURSERY SCHOOL – 1974**

*Back Row:* Duncan Macpherson, Dillon Kennedy.

*1st Row:* Paul Modet, Helmer Adams, Priya Rana, James Strauss, James Hyman, Eugenie Livanos, Nicholas Konialidis, Charles Kinross, Veronique Bourgeois, Jonathan Pyser.

*2nd Row:* Rupert Morison, Tobie Williams, Matthew Johns, Elinor Ball, William Bethell, James Lengemann, Hannah Garrard, Philip Flaccomio.

*3rd Row:* Alexander Beeber, Jasmine Lassen, Alisa Modet, Peter Manley, Angela Reissmann, Patrick Donovan, Cynthia Stellakis, Stephen Pace, Rachel Margolis, Simone Wakwella, Daniel Gold, Katherine Kinross, David Duboff, Nicholas Gold, Scott Garfield.

*4th Row:* Alexis Albion, Paul Sellar, Laura Solomons, Jason Simpson, Kristin Paulyson, Christopher St. Geroge, Leonore Sharp, Shanna Langdon, Lee Freeman, Michelle Pena, Nicolas Beitner, Melanie Hutchins.

*5th Row:* Henrietta Baldock, Rachel Aguilo, David Cannon, Beverly Anne Langford, Benjamin Wigram, Amanda Simpson, Toby Strauss, Charlotte Lurot, Guy Maitland-Smith, Alexandra Ashbourne, Johnne Karki, Tracy Garfield, Laura Nilsen.

**HYDE PARK NURSERY SCHOOL – 1975**

*Back Row*: Elinor Ball, James Hyman, Eugine Livanos.

*2nd Row*: Leonore Sharp, Benjamin Wigram, Laura Solomons, Toby Strauss, Nicholas Beitner, Pruiya Rana, Justin Nash, Beverly Anne Langford.

*3rd Row*: Michelle Pena, Paul Sellar, Kristin Paulyson, Jasmine Lassen, Georgina Frost, Lance Malmgren, Angela Reissman.

*4th Row*: Marisa Collings, Lara Abu, Nowar Hanan, Allaf Kirsteen Deeves, Nicole Garcia, George Loverdos, David Duboff, Danielle Roffe, Maria Ioannou, Henrietta Baldock, Charles Lyon, Alexandra Ashbourne, Waleed Mondani, Shanna Langdon.

*5th Row*: Dylan Farr, Ambereen Yusof, Johnne Karki, Andrea Johnson, Nicholas Gold, Samantha Angus, Isabelle Favre, Lucy Phillips, Tristan Simmonds, Poline Lemos, Sandeep Jain, Suzanne Calvo, Luke Lockhart.

*6th Row*: Jason Power, Charlotte Lurot, Gregory Hunter, Cindy Davies, Saskia Thornton, Julian Lee, Rachel Troostwyck, Toby Walker, Sarah Lloyd, Mark Kessler, Mona Alladin.

*Front Row*: Dolores Abbott, James Hanscombe, Huda Allaf, Rachel Aguilo, James Fellowes, Tracy Garfield, Gareth Langdon, Alexandra Papageorghiou, Simon Johns, Victoria Frost, Christos Ioannou, Vanessa Mason, James Ker-Lindsay, Karyn von Mattiesen.

## HYDE PARK NURSERY SCHOOL – SUMMER 1976

*Back Row:* Miss Karen, Mrs Kay, Miss Penny, Mrs Doreen, Miss Una, Miss Dawn

*2nd Row:* Saskia Thornton, David Jones, Fotini Efthimiou, Camilia Farah, Tristan Simmonds, Huda Allaf, Garath Langdon, Rachel Troostwyk, Hanan Allaf, Nicholas Gold, Catriona Macdonald, Mark Kessler, Poline Lemos, James Fellowes.

*3rd Row:* Duncan McGrath, Nicholas Walter, Yvette Crompton, Gregory Palmer, Kelly Sinclair, Julian Marks, Victoria Frost, James Hanscombe, Alexandra Papageorghiou, Mark Michaels, Jagrati Jain, Paras Chandaria, Joanna Barnett, John Louis Rios, Colete St Clair, Adam Perry.

*4th Row:* Marc Asseily, Samantha Angus, Amar Eryani, Karyn von Matthiessen, Murrough O'Brien, Rachel Aguilo, Toby Walker, Karen McGrath, Sandeep Jain, Sarah Lloyd, Luke Lockhart, Cynthia Davis.

*Front Row:* Shaheen Yusuf, Geno Choucair, Christina Pardal, Paul Briggs, Natalie Salvatori, Michael Hanania, Mary Ellen Donovan, Charles Fellowes, Gemma Deeves, Fabian Sharp, Samantha Nix, Daniel Wray, Aanal Chandaria, Matthiew Brener, Katerina Efthimiou.

## HYDE PARK NURSERY SCHOOL – SUMMER 1977

*Back Row:* Miss Carol, Mrs Doreen, Mrs Kay, Mrs Lucinda, Miss Aileen, Miss Karen.

*2nd Row:* Karyn von Matthiessen, Gregory Palmer, Tamara Gatward, Mark Michaels, Hanan Allaf, Jimmy Kesruani, Huda Allaf, John Louis Rios, Kate Saunders, Daminic Whiting, Jagrati Jain, John-Kenneth Closs, Paul Briggs.

*3rd Row:* Rachel Troostwyk, Alexander Massey, Joanna Meyer, Vishal Patrao, Amanda Miller, Shah Haider, Sophia Jundi, Nicholas Gold, Sahavet Soufraki, Harry Rambaut, Rania Shams, Duncan McGrath, Yvette Crompton, Luke Lockhart, Nicholas Walter, Natalie Salvatori, Damian Rayne, Joanna Barnett.

*4th Row:* Jo Kesruani, Alexia Kleonakos, Fabian Sharp, Kelly Sinclair, Geno Choucair, Katerina Efthimiou, Charles Fellowes, Samantha Nix, Matthew Brener, Victoria Tompkins, Julian Marks, Dina Tayara.

*5th Row:* Deborah Wolfson, Alexander Edmonds, Christima Pardal, Daniel Wray, Gemma Deeves, Lucy Constantini, Pandelis Lemos, Lara Masters, Aanal Chandaria, Mary Ellen Donovan, Nabil Soufraki.

*Front Row:* Leonie Schroder, Natasha Roffe, Andrew Williams, Damian Angus, Hanouf Al-Majed, Samuel Parkes, Charlotte Polizzi, Mario Nuzzo, Fletcher Horobin.

# HYDE PARK NURSERY SCHOOL – SUMMER 1978

*Back Row:* Gilad Yakov, Miss Aline, Miss Pat, Mrs Kay, Mrs Lucinda, Miss Gillian, Miss Carol, Severine Teurlai.

*4th Row:* Victoria Tompkins, Johnny di Francise, Yvette Crompton, Jerome Pinsent, Lucy Constantini, John-Kenneth Closs, Deborah Wolfson, Pandelis Lemos, Kate Saunders, Mohammed Taha, Abeer Baadarani, Jean-Jacque Lorraine, Lara Masters, Roland Glasser.

*3rd Row:* Natasha Roffe, Sam Parkes, Genna Preston, Damian Angus, Laura Walsh, Daniel Wray, Christina Pardal, Shah Halder, Gayle Robertson, Sergio Beggiato, Katerina Efthimiou, Alexander Edmonds, Gemma Deeves, Damian Rayne, Camilla Marcel.

*2nd Row:* Robert Ritter, Hanouf Al-Majed, Danny Yefet, Claire Gold, Jason Simmonds, Poppy Lilley, Daniel Kessler, Angelique Swanepoel, Brenton Battenfeld, Muna Wehbe, Fletcher Horobin, Eleanor Riddell, Ahmed Moharram, Kate Loustau-Lalanne, Alex Telnikoff.

*Front Row:* Oliver Bedack, Mark Parkinson, Maya Tayara, Lujo Besker, Guy Lorraine, Mark Kikano, Oliver Provenza, Shujon Khan, Rabea Baadarani, James Walter, Alexander Nix, Michael Nott, Ali Mohanna, Taymour Polding.

## HYDE PARK NURSERY SCHOOL – SUMMER 1979

*Back Row:* Miss Philippa, Mrs Aline, Mrs Kay, Lady Colville, Miss Sue, Miss Debbie.

*4th Row:* Ahmed Moharram, Baron Bloom, Michael Nott, Julian Soper, David Ginsberg, Camilla Marcel, Damian Rayne, Muna Wehbe, Oliver Provenza, Brenton Battenfeld, Oliver Bedack, Mark Kikano, Alex Telnikoff, Daniel Kessler, Damion Angus, Fletcher Horobin.

*3rd Row:* James Walter, Taymour Polding, Beverley Ann Bloom, Ali Mohanna, Severine Teurlai, Dorian Delap, Claire Gold, Alexander Nix, Maya Tayara, Maxwell Shillinglaw, Sereen Daou, Michael Geha, Fleur Brener, Rami Ghandour, Tamara Brovat, David Sikes, Lujo Bauer.

*2nd Row:* Christina Pardal, Harry Chan, Danah Yassin, Oliver Lurot, Marika Lemos, Alexander Asseily, Kate Loustau-Lalanne, Luke Leander, Miranda Glasser, Peter Lawn, Polly McCowan, George Vlotides.

*Front Row:* Sam Gordon, Chloe Lilley, Robert Soper, Rebecca Katrein, Andrew Murdock, May Yassin, Stuart Rowe, Claudia Massey, Nathaniel Schooler, Xenia Lemos, Alexander Gatward, Poppy Lilley.

# HYDE PARK NURSERY SCHOOL – SUMMER 1980

*Back Row:* Bertie Nix, Arrianna Hohenlohe, Nathaniel Schooler.

*4th Row:* Mrs. Molly, Miss Jane, Lady Colville, Robert Soper, Miranda Glasser, Maggie McCown, Luke Leander, Tamara Fogel, Stuart Rowe, Sereen Daou, James Bussell, Miss Debbie, Miss Philippa, Mrs. Kay.

*3rd Row:* Shalini Varma, Kunal Bijlani, Simon Vasco, Xenia Lemos, Max Shillinglaw, David Hadj, Rhona Clelland, Tariq Al-Khater, Bibi Korvalian, Daniel Weston, Polly McCowen, Rudy Leander, Genna Preston, Lugo Bauer, Beverley Ann Bloom, Terrell Cole, Marika Lemos, Kate Loustau-Lalanne, Sufian Al-Mukhtar.

*2nd Row:* Nino Constantini, Radha Kapoor, Nicholas Johnson, Sophia Heng, Oliver Lurot, Danielle Crompton, Rami Ghandour, Christina Ritter, Mark Parkinson, Shayma Al-Mashat, Demitris Efthymiou, Antoinette Fernandez, Feisal Gwaderi.

*Front Row:* Dorian Delap, Thomas Northcliffe, Nicholas Ginsberg, Lee Mohlere, Rupert Willats, Anatasia Feifer, David Brim, Claudia Massey, Harley Mckinley, Katy Roth, William Mills, Alexndra Townsley, Stefan Hanania.

he marched the regiment from Aberdeen to Inverness across the Cairngorms she came up from the Dee where she was fishing to see them go past – a hugely appreciated gesture.

Nicholas and Emma Bourne of the Bourne and Hollingsworth family, the Murdoch children Andrew and Elizabeth, Carl Foreman's Amanda and Jonathan all brought parent variety and interest to our lives, as did many others who appear elsewhere in my story.

Irene Cleveland, grand-daughter of an American President, and Reggie Maudling's grandchild, together with Helena Ten Bos, Marina, Arieta, Eugenie and Stavros Livanos, Charles and James Fellows, James and Thomas Profumo, Deborah Wolfson, Joanna and Genna Preston, whose father headed up Macdonalds in Europe . . . I could go on for ever, because the parents were fun and the children were my life.

# CHAPTER FOUR

With seventy children divided between St. John's Church Hall, our house at Somers Crescent, and my Sister's top floor in Hyde Park Crescent, we were bursting at the seams. I had been for some time talking over the problem with John Hollamby, Chesterton's top man for the area on behalf of the Church Commissioners. John is an internationally known yachtsman who has sailed in the formidable Admiral's Cup and Fastnet Races. A real charmer, full of wit and humour, he was a strong supporter of the School and a loyal ally to me. One day he stopped me in the street and said "I think I've got a solution for you – come and see". I went and saw. At first my heart sank, then I became enthusiastic over the potential.

We had gone to St. George's Fields, a square area bounded by Bayswater Road, Albion Street, Connaught Street and Archery Close. There some rather ugly blocks of flats had been built by the Utopian Housing Association on the historic land belonging to St. George's, Hanover Square, and one strip five hundred feet long by fifty feet wide, running east to west behind Connaught Street, had been used as the builder's yard and was now vacant. The owners of the flats ceded it to the Church Commissioners in return for road access on to Albion Street. Chesterton's at that time had a vague idea of making it a through road, or possibly a new mews, but in the forseeable future it was empty. This was offered to me for my own and the School's purposes only, at an initial licence fee of £100 a year which Chesterton's increased tenfold when I had established the garden.

The area was not just not vacant, it was derelict. The east end had a few war-time allotments, abandoned and overgrown. The rest was churned up by contractor's plant, littered with debris dating back to bombs which had contributed broken glass in profusion, and dotted with tombstones, whole and broken. It had been a graveyard and remained such until 1868, then it was closed.

St. George's Church had granted permission in 1857 to the Nuns of the Poor Clare Order to occupy the south east corner. It is a closed order whose lives are devoted to praying for London and its people. The order was founded by Totteridge born Cardinal Manning of my husband's college of Trinity, Oxford, and the Nuns are followers of Clare of Assisi. Clare was seventeen when she heard St. Francis of Assisi preach in 1212 and realised that by stepping aside from the world, she would have a greater perspective to help others. The Nuns came over to Westminster from Belgium and to this day their sole contact with the outside world is by correspondence. The Mother Abbess tells me the Nuns keep in touch by selected newspaper clippings displayed on their notice board. When they returned to their rebuilt convent in 1970 there were thirty four nuns and since then the numbers have fluctuated. They are helpful and kind neighbours.

When the flats were being built there were still the coffins, six deep in places, one on top of the other. Some of the bottom ones, of great antiquity, were made of lead. After the proper rites had been observed, the bulldozers moved in and the dumper trucks whisked away the debris through the streets occasionally, I regret to impart, shedding the odd human bone as they bumped round the corners!

When we started to use the grounds as a play area we erected a swing for the children. One day we noticed the swings were no longer safe as they had tilted badly. On checking what was wrong we discovered that one of the coffins had caved in. We brought it to the Church Commissioners' attention as this was the statutory procedure. We had to have a service of reburial for the coffin. We placed a notice in the newspaper, as we knew by the number on the lid of the coffin and by the records of deaths kept by St. George's Church who the person was. It then had to be sent to a mortuary, a Church service held and the coffin reburied. This was an expensive and time consuming exercise. The outcome of this episode was if a coffin did appear near the surface we very carefully checked its position and very slowly moved it sideways always nine inches below ground level to make sure we did not have to go over the whole proceedings again.

We did not have these difficulties subsequently as we erected only light classroom structures. But all that was some time ahead, and first I faced the huge challenge of creating a garden out of dereliction. The first phase dealt with all except the old allotments at the far end from the Albion Street entrance. The Keyes Brothers, whose uncle Colonel Geoffrey Keyes won a V.C. in the raid to capture The German Field Marshall Rommel for which Tommy was Adjutant during the second world war, undertook the task. After much effort Clifton Nurseries in Warwick Way made a really beautiful blend of lawns, shrubs, trees and flag-stoned play areas. An added feature is the loan from my twin sister of the lovely old stone horsetrough from the Hyde Park Crescent taxi rank, horse drawn in yesteryear, which holds throughout the year a colourful show of flowers. Another is from the disused Presbyterian Church of St. James's, Dulwich in South London, a beautiful stone font on its pedestal which is now a bird bath.

The builder's yard took much hard work to turn into a safe garden, as well as a beautiful one. Another solution was found as satisfactory as it was surprising. Mrs. Pat Rambaut had Andrew and Harry at the school and her children were collected most days by Mrs. Tinkler, who looked after the Rambaut's house whilst Mrs. Rambaut spent much time professionally checking the script and continuity of such films as "The City of Joy" and "Wuthering Heights". Andrew is now a zoology student at Edinburgh University after leaving us for the Dragon School, Oxford and Gordonstoun and Harry is at Gwent reading fine art. Pat and I met in the school garden and she mentioned the nervous illness from which Mr. Tinkler was suffering and asked if he and his family could come at week-ends to enjoy its peace as most of his troubles were, according to him, put down to the noise on the Lisson Grove Estate. They came with children, grandchildren and picnics – the broken glass in every inch of the ground, a left over relic of the wartime bombing, was collected. The overgrown vegetable garden, started in the First

World War when "Dig for Britain" was the slogan and fertile soil had been mixed with the solid clay, was restored to fertility for rhubarb, peas and beans. No plants were bought, seeds covered with plastic became seedlings, and planted out amongst the trees and shrubs. Colour and beauty abounded. The Westminster City Council finally exchanged the Tinklers' flat for a house in the country where I am sure he has made a beautiful garden because his creative talents did so much for us. Mrs. Carl Taylor, a senior gardener for Connaught Village took over, and on her mother's death Bill Murtagh her father, a retired butcher continued the good work.

But the school needed more than a playground, and we were not allowed to erect any buildings. After much pleading for the absolute requirement of a reception, secretarial and first aid centre, a small wooden building was allowed near the solid oak gates.

We looked for classroom space in the houses in Connaught Street which backed onto the Garden. In almost all the ground floor was designated for shop use and could not be changed, and the shops were all occupied except Number 31. John Hollamby enabled us to get the lease, which was rack-rented, and to find a tenant for the shop who, together with a statutory tenant in the top two floors, virtually paid the outgoings – except for a nasty but fortunately one-off problem with an external chimney on the party wall. We were left with two rooms, one semi-basement and the other above it, opening onto our garden. These measured seventeen feet by fifteen feet. They were light and airy and ideal for classrooms, and on the inner side of the lower one we added the inevitably necessary lavatories for children and staff. This was still not enough, and after many tentative contacts with the Connaught Street neighbours we were able to form a trouble-free link with Mr. Leach of New Holland Publishing Ltd., the bookshop at Number 39. We converted their ground floor rear storeroom into a classroom and added lavatories – yes, more! Then we built on to it on the garden side a curved roofed elegant glass extension, the only type of construction we were permitted, and this was all christened the Bookroom.

The whole result was a fabulous garden for children and a pleasure for neighbours to see.

Kay Evans took over the care of the two year olds in the Bookroom. She was there for some years, quiet and competent until the creche was started and she moved up to the Gate House classroom. Charles Cholmondeley, Christopher Gregory, Neil Inglis, Lucy Edwards, Gavin Tucker, and Chester Chipperfield I remember there. Kay has married and continues on the staff of Ravenstone House, the versatile and hard working Michelle Lutchford joining her in 1989.

John Hollamby came round and smiled his approval. He said "You know, I offered you this tongue-in-cheek. I never thought you would achieve what you have".

Our garden is surrounded by a double wall forming a walk-way just wide enough for a man to walk swinging a truncheon like a baseball bat. It is called the Body Snatchers' Walk, and was a relic of the late Victorian days of Burke and Hare, when body snatchers robbed new graves and sold the bodies to hospitals for dissection for research and medical teaching.

I wanted to do something about the old gravestones scattered about, and I obtained authorisation for a Manpower Services Group for this work with the help of the Senior District Occupational Therapist of St. Mary's Hospital, Paddington, Miss Vanona Keans, as my referee. She knew of our work, our need for premises and how to fill in all the many forms. This involved me in going on a week's course in Clerkenwell to qualify as a Manpower Services Manager! An extra bonus was that we were allowed for this project to erect another self-contained building, down on the old allotments. My husband got hold of an attractive and solid prefabricated wooden structure, and the way-leave we had to negotiate for the sewer connection proved invaluable when, much later, our real expansion began. In return for repaving and painting the tiny yard of the Hairdressers, Mr. Pascal Chevalier courteously allowed us sewer access. The Manpower Service Scheme to help young unemployed was viewed with great suspicion by the Trade Unions and could only undertake work with no conceivable profit motive. That was certainly the case with moving and cataloguing hundreds of gravestones. The shattered ones went away in a series of skips, and the others, to comply with safety regulations, had to be laid flat and carefully matched into a pattern, or firmly fixed against the outer wall. Each one was numbered and catalogued – including one which, with body snatchers in mind, was engraved with a curse on anyone who disturbed it – and the catalogue went to the previous owners, St. George's Church, Hanover Square.

The Rector there, The Reverend W.A. Atkins, is a good friend to the School and the Charity, and he wrote me so fascinating a letter about the history of the place that I reproduce it here.

"The sale of our burial ground started a long time ago when the Church Commissioners offered us £20,000 for the land. As you know the streets on all three sides of the ground belonged to the Church Commissioners and they wanted it to be integrated. At that moment in time there was nowhere for me to live within the Parish, I said that it was a ridiculously small sum as it would not buy me anywhere to live and so I turned down the offer. The word got around that there was the possibility of the ground becoming available. We were approached by a gentlemen who offered us £125,000. My Church Warden and I decided that if it was worth that amount to this old boy, it must be worth considerably more to us. We then had the business of entertaining offers. All kinds of people entertained us to lunches in the most lavish way and it was enormous fun. The main stumbling block was that planning permission had been blocked initially, oddly enough, by the Church Commissioners. Fortunately my Church Warden had two brothers-in-law who were Church Commissioners and they weighed in against the Estate Secretary and freed us from this objection and so we carried on with the offers still coming in.

We obtained Planning Permission and then we had to have an Act of Parliament passed. All the negotiations and hearings took almost twelve years, from 1968 to 1980, until we obtained full permission which enabled us to sell. At that time we had an agreement with the Diocese, by which they should receive half the proceeds from any sale from the ground, a quarter to the Parish for endowment and restoration of the Church, and a quarter to the Hyde Park Estate Trust.

The Trust was already in existence but had a very minimal income. This was derived from the houses on the Bayswater Road. They were all tied up in long leases with small rents coming in, so we were a poverty stricken little Charity. After the Act of Parliament the sale went through. We then re-formed the Trusts, and contacted the Charity Commissioners as they had devised an entirely new scheme for Charities. The scope of the Civil Trust, which is the one we deal with educationally, covers Westminster City Council boundaries, a much larger area than it did when it was originally created for those living within the Parish. Westminster now embraces Paddington and Marylebone as well as the old Westminster. These increased funds, instead of being plentiful, have become over-stretched. The Commissioners agreed in the end to allow the use of our land for the new development of social welfare single people homes. We sacrificed a strip of land on the North side in return for vehicular access to Albion Street. It became the home of the Hyde Park School. There was talk of building a row of mews houses there, or an access road for the Connaught Street shops. The main area was sold to property developers called Utopian Housing Corporation who I believe are selling off the free-holds of these little flats. They were originally meant as small family units, in fact the very children we are funding so frequently in Hyde Park School and St. George's School. I think the Utopian people had the right idea at the time. There was plenty of provision in Peabody Buildings for people of the working class, but those of modest income and the middle classes who were working in London had no provision made for them to live anywhere in the city. The idea was that those in this category would be able to afford to live near their jobs and I think it was a splendid idea.

It was the Church Wardens of St. George's Hanover Square who sold the ground and not the Church Commissioners. The Wardens were directly responsible for the land. There was never any query raised as to whether it was sold on the inner or outer wall boundary. I think it was on the inner boundary wall as between was a freeway until the bombs came in 1940. The reason for the outer wall was to frustrate grave robbers. People used to nip over the graveyard wall and exhume recently buried bodies and these would end up on the dissecting tables of London hospitals.

This happened to Lawrence Stern. Some of his friends were invited to witness such a dissection when they suddenly realised that the body on the operating table was their old friend. Lawrence Stern had been the Rector of Coxwold in Yorkshire but did not live there all the time. He had a house at the bottom of George Street, hence his being interred in the Parish Burial Ground. The next decision made was that we should have a Watchman and a Watch House was built at the Bayswater entrance to the Burial Ground. They constructed this double walled walk-way so the Watchman could parade every so often and it would deter grave robbers, who would have to carry the bodies over two walls instead of one. The whole place was badly churned up during the First World War, most of the grave-stones were removed in order to "Dig for Victory". During the Second World War two high explosive devices landed on the land and again churned it rather badly.

Permission was granted in 1944 to an Archery club for three acres for toxophily as they had previously used the ground until 1734. The Nurses from St. Mary's Hospital had part for use as tennis courts and Sir Arthur Bryant, who lived in Archery Close, had a small plot where he grew the most beautiful flowers. The north piece of land was not sold but given to the Church Commissioners who in return gave permission for development and access. This was a convenience for the people living along the North side too. It was a great relief when the Bill went through Parliament. We had great fun and enlisted the help of Wing Commander Bullis, M.P., on the Conservative side and a very good Scotsman called Mr McConnel, an M.P. on the Labour side to back us. It was just as well that we had both sides sympathetic to what we wanted to do. On the other side we came up against some very heavy artillery in Lady Joan Vickers, who opposed us like anything, and a rather strange individual from the Labour side whose name I cannot recall. Joan Vickers wanted to protect the Albion Street dwellers from having the beautiful view from their windows abolished, the Labour M.P. wanted it to be become a children's playground and also a Primary School.

St. George's Fields are still part of our Parish. There was a question about Marriage Banns. Someone had gone to the Vicar of St. John's in Hyde Park Crescent, which is nearer and asked for their banns to be posted. Unknown to him the girl concerned came to us and said they were in the Parish of St. George, Hanover Square and would we call the banns. These banns were therefore called twice and this caused quite an anomaly. I mentioned this to Gerald Ellison who was the Bishop of London at the time and suggested we had better re-organise the Parish boundaries and restore the St. George's Field Estate to St. John's Church in Hyde Park Crescent. He said "Don't try and disturb anything, it will be a meal for the lawyers", so we let it rest.

Probably the most famous of all the St. George's parishioners was George Frederick Handel, the celebrated composer. He came to live in Brook Street in 1724 and it was there that he wrote his most famous work "The Messiah". He worshipped at the Church for thirty five years until his death in 1759. Among the prominent people who were Rectors was Robert Hodgson in 1803. Through the marriage of his grand-daughter to the Earl of

Strathmore, he became an ancestor of our present Queen.

Prince Augustus Frederick, Duke of Sussex, sixth son of King George III, married Lady Augusta Murray, daughter of the Earl of Dunmore. They had wed secretly in Rome on April the fifth 1793. When they returned to England they were married at St. George's again. They had not received the Royal Consent and the marriage was annulled in the summer of 1794.

The Duke of Kingston married Elizabeth Chudleigh in 1769. Unfortunately she was already married to Augustus John Hervey, later the third Earl of Bristol. Tried for bigamy by the Peers in 1776 she was found guilty and retired to the Continent. Other well known people to be married in St. George's were:- Joseph Grimaldi the actor, P.B. Shelley, George Eliot, Lord Alfred Douglas of Oscar Wilde fame and the author John Buchan, as well as the politicians Benjamin Disraeli and Theodore (Teddy) Roosevelt, the future President of the United States of America. Gugielmo Marconi, the inventor of the wireless telegraph, also appears on the Marriage Register following his wedding to the daughter of Lord Inchiquin on the sixteenth of March, 1905.

In the nineteenth century nearly all of the education stemmed from the churches of London. I am not certain whether it was all over Great Britain, but in London they had a firm grip on all forms of education. As you can see from the book that has been published St. George's had fingers in a lot of educational pies.

It was at one time a most powerful Church. In the 17th century it had been ceded from St. Martin-in-the-Fields. St. Martin's boundaries had been reduced with the coming of King James the Sixth of Scotland and First of England. King James brought his court down to just east of St. Martin's and brought with him the Scottish Church called the Crown Court in Covent Garden and a Police Force with a headquarters called Scotland Yard, to protect the Court and St. James's Palace."

Hyde Park School was building up the qualified teaching staff and also a very stable auxiliary team – all important to the administrative side. Napoleon's army marched on its stomach, they say. Nursery Schools advance on spotless cleanliness, proper diet and regular time-tables.

In 1970 Margaret Hemsley came into our lives to join Ester. She had been the house-keeper to the famous architect Sir Robert Matthew until he retired and went to live in the country having sold his Regent's Park house. Margaret was an Aberdonian, gruff and forthright but very kind, full of humour, and a hard worker with high standards. She moved into the garden level flat at Somers Crescent with her Greek husband, a beautiful daughter called Nicola and a sheep dog called Nicholas. These rooms included a living room with big French windows into the garden. They settled there happily until her untimely and sudden departure. She died in Ester's arms one morning whilst having a mug of tea, suffering a massive haemorrhage. For her it was a happy way to go, for us it was the loss of a real friend. The end was indeed sudden, she had been with us for fifteen years. Her husband remained a further six months until he found a place near his daughter, Nicola, and her husband.

Margaret and Ester worked in partnership and the growing School needed the two of them. The stores were bought wholesale and stored in the larder or bought at Mrs. Sells of Fuller's Stores at 14 Porchester Place. The two of them were known as "The Halt and The Deaf". Ester was so deaf that she could not hear the doorbell or the telephone. Margaret was so lame that she took ages to reach the door or telephone. It served to decrease mobility which sometimes was not a bad thing for nursery life is made up of a myriad of minor queries and the need to be constantly present.

The food was delivered to the classrooms on trolleys. The first year the lunches were served in the hall and when we had to leave the hall for modernisation, the rear of the Connaught Street house with its massive flying buttress, was available and the children ate in their classrooms. It was not until the completion of the new building in 1987, that all the cooking was transferred to the new purpose built kitchen. From the day Margaret died we stopped cooking at home. Andreanoff, a family Delicatessen shop at 65 Connaught Street, came to our help. Mark Andreanoff runs the business cheerfully and competently with Andy and Mary. Andy, a trained cook, was in charge of our meals. Catering for between thirty and forty meals became burdensome with bumpy unsprung trolleys, so it was a great pleasure when the kitchen was finally available for use. We did resist parents offering to bring in sandwiches. It was not a question of not wanting the parents to spoil their young but at that age children cannot comprehend why one person's plate is a different colour from someone else's. We were trying to avoid odious comparisons of any kind.

Our younger son Duncan was soon to join the school. He and Balavil came at the same time and their lives have been intertwined. At times I think they vied to see which one could give the most problems!

The grey bulk of Balavil dominates the Spey Valley in the Clan Macpherson country between Kingussie and Kincraig. It takes little imagination to envisage the long history of the site and the many generations that have looked down on the river.

Standing stones in the area and cave dwellings indicate a very early civilisation. Later, we know the Picts lived here, and there is a theory that their King lived on the mound where Balavil stands. There was a Pictish Kingdom and King about every twenty five miles up and down the valley.

The meadow below the house was long ago called Kings Park and there is a hill behind the house called King Hara's where the watchman and his beacon stood as sentinels to warn the tribe. If danger was imminent they withdrew men, women, children, cattle and dogs to the fort whose traces lie on the Balavil – Dunachton march. At that time the danger came by water, up the broader River Spey, where the Vikings, who had settled on the shores of the Moray Firth, rowed their shallow longboats to raid for what they lacked, wives and cattle.

Time passed, and between the eleventh and thirteenth centuries the forebears of the Macphersons arrived in Badenoch from the west.

The Comyns were the Lords of Badenoch, with a seat at Ruthven and a second fortified house on or near the site of Balavil. Many tales are handed down of their brutality and greed, and when Robert Bruce contested the throne of Scotland with the house of Comyn, the Sons of the Cat were only too glad to rise against the hated overlord. The hand holding a dagger in the Macpherson coat of arms celebrates the success of the Bruce cause, and particularly, if less appropriately, the murder of the Red Comyn.

Gradually the Macphersons, their name established from the celebrated Murdoch parson of Kingussie, came to dominate the Upper Spey Valley, and their mastery was sealed by the slaughter of the MacNiven warriors trapped at Raitts.

Raitts was the early name of the Balavil village and stronghold, with the low ground often referred to, in the Mackintosh records, as Chapelpark. The latter came from the 12th century chapel, now on Dunachton ground, which is the re-build of a foundation by a disciple of St. Columba, St. Malcolm.

The Clan Mackintosh twice occupied the house on the Balavil site for considerable periods, through marriage to the heiress. The first period was in the 16th century, and we discovered among some rubble a stone carved with the coat of arms identified as those of Lachlan Mackintosh, who became Chief of the Clan about 1564.

The second Mackintosh occupation, early in the 18th century, was more dramatic. Lachlan of the 16th century was known as Lachlan the Good. The Mackintoshs of Borlum were definitely "bad". Fathers and sons were notorious and violent men. Finally they made a bold and unsuccessful attempt in 1743 to kidnap for ransom Duncan Forbes of Culloden, Lord President of the Council of Scotland, near the Gynack on General Wade's new road. They were recognised and later arrested, and as part of the punishment their fortified house at Raitts, now Balavil, was raised to the ground.

Resurrection came with James Macpherson, who made his name from the Ossian epic poems that sparked the romantic revival, and his fortune from London dealings on behalf of an Indian potentate. Member of Parliament for the Borough of Camelford and an associate of Pitt, he had friends in high places through whom he negotiated the return of the exiled Chief of the Clan and the re-purchase of the estates, emerging himself with the rich lands of Glenbanchor and Chapelpark. The elegant old house at Chapelpark, sadly no longer there, was his home, and there he entertained the great figures of Edinburgh's intellectual society, such as Adam

Smith, the father of modern economics, Robertson the historian, David Hume the philosopher and the Adam brothers of whom Robert was to design and build the new house at Balavil.

You can imagine them in brilliant conversation lasting far into the night, the bottles on the table and the long-stemmed white clay pipes in their mouths. These small bowled pipes kept going out, and they would rise to re-light them from the glowing peat in the hearth. As the level in the bottles sank lower and their legs grew heavier, sometimes a turf of peat was put on the table, burning side up. Occasionally it was forgotten at the end, and the mahogany table where they sat, which we have, has today a piece cut into it to replace an area that was charred.

Robert Adam duly built James's new house, with its front door at the back of the design, opening right on to General Wade's new highway, and James called it Belleville in then French style, but also probably punning on the Gaelic "Place of the Sacred Oak" (Baile a Bhil).

In Victorian times, with shooting parties all the rage, the east wing was added in two rather untidy phases. A fire in 1900 damaged the entrance porch, the hall and the gallery, and during restoration bay windows were added at the front. About 1920 the west wing was added in brick, and this we had to pull down in 1970 as it was in a dangerous condition.

James Macpherson had five children by three ladies, none of whom he married. He was succeeded in Balavil by his son James, and in her book "Memoirs of a Highland Lady" Mrs. Grant shows he and his wife were a charming young couple who were popular in the social scene, then dominated by the Duchess of Gordon at Kinrara. Alas, they died young and without issue, as did all James' family save one sister. She married David Brewster, later to be Sir David who invented the kaleidoscope and was one of the founders of the British Association for the Advancement of Science. He had been helping to manage the Balavil Estate, and to his love of trees we owe the original great planting in the policies, including a Wellingtonia and the first Canadian Douglas Fir to be planted in Scotland.

The next generation, to comply with the stringent hereditary conditions of James's will, took the name Brewster-Macpherson. The second of that line, Charles J.B. lost an arm in an accident early in life but nevertheless became a noted stag and big game shot. His elder son was killed in the 1914 war. His younger son, sadly, succeeded his father only briefly. He left a widow, the late Mrs. Peggy Brewster-Macpherson of Balavil, resident at Lynchat. She had no children. So the line of James "Ossian" Macpherson has died out, except for the descendants of C.J.B.'s two sisters, the notable Scottish families of Butter and Baxter.

Balavil was briefly occupied by the Military during the second War and much damage was done. The house was then abandoned and fell into decay. The private gas supply, made by a primitive but efficient device in the grounds, collapsed, and there had of course never been electricity. The water supply from the hill disappeared under the roots of new forestry. Huge holes appeared in eaves and floors and the house perished with rot. A capercailzie flew through a main window and lay dead on the floor of the salon and there was not a stick of furniture.

Restoration, was it folly or courage? was certainly a labour of love and a long and laborious one. We took on a lease from the Trustees of James "Ossian" Macpherson's estate. Now this great house of Balavil stands in its pristine Regency glory, and we are certainly proud of what we have achieved. The decorations inside were restored over a period of three winters by the work of Douglas Mackintosh of Newtonmore, under my husband's detailed guidance. Theirs was an old partnership, as Douglas had been his orderly early in the war, in the Queen's Own Cameron Highlanders.

There was enough space on the top floor to convert the rooms at the top of the Victorian tower staircase into a flat. The McBeths inhabited this first. His great gardening gifts have now taken him to a senior position in the Botanical Gardens in Edinburgh, and it was he who started to work on our garden.

The muddy moorland around the house has been turned into tiered lawns of great elegance by Robbie Gair and they have been edged with road-side paving stones. The remainder is gravel, easy to keep, and Robbie is still its guardian. He was born on the estate in the spacious pre-war days and has lived there all his life. Animals follow him as if he were the Pied Piper!

The Whites next took over the flat. Johnny was the signalman at Kingussie Station, and was our guide and helper with all our many rail journeys. His wife, Helen, a Macpherson by birth, was delighted to be back in the heart of Clan country.

Duncan grew up there, a much wanted and treasured possession, helping feed our black Labradors, Kudu and her daughter Cailleach, as well as Ruara, Morag and Shona, the Shetland sheepdogs who travelled to and from London with us. By the end of 1971 most of the major work had been completed and Mrs. Margaret Cameron joined the domestic team. We both attended the church in Newtonmore and have officer sons serving in the British Army.

The house had never known electricity and the water supply from the hill was irreparably damaged. Duncan made his first visit at Easter. To heat the old building Captain Lindsay had lent us radiators and along with ours a warm glow greeted us. In the middle of the night an enormous bang shook the house. Marion Hall grabbed Duncan and we met on the landing. "It's only a piece of the west wing we're demolishing which has fallen," I said comfortingly. "Then why is it glowing red over there?" she replied, pointing to the garage, where the main electricity cable entered the house. She was right, the electricity had failed. I rang Malcolm Innes, the Newtonmore electrician who replied, "Yes and there's no electricity in Kingussie, Newtonmore, Dalwhinnie or the Upper Spey Valley". Very few of the local residents have forgotten the day electricity came to Balavil.

Marion and Ishbel shared a love of horses and Marion added a love of her driving instructor. She moved over in due course to Miss Georgie Henschell's renowned riding school and two years later married her instructor.

By now Duncan and I had worked out a special partnership and when parents came for interviews, he would happily use his play-pen beside me in the spacious Somers Crescent house. Occasionally he slipped from grace, once marching naked to my side and turning to a prospective pupil aged all of three weeks, crying "Milk Milk" and holding out a large bottle of Whisky. They never came back!

Duncan and I went to Ireland with Tommy and we stayed at Castle Martin, with Tony and Susan O'Reilly. Tony was a celebrated Ireland and British Lions rugger player, celebrated raconteur, and celebrated business man who has become the worldwide chief of the Heinz company. This was to be the first of many happy short trips we were to make together, trying to keep up with his father, to Monaco, Nantes, Italy and Wales, to name but a few.

The longer holidays at Balavil were a haven for children and found me in my element. Will and James Bethell and their mother Tiggie Lady Bethell, Laura Jane and Emma Louise Ogilvy and Roger and Moyra Bannister's daughter Erin all stayed with us. The house was filling with furniture as well as people. Both the Drakes at Inshriach and Gilmours at Montraive emptied their beautiful homes at that time and sold to us large solid practical furniture which continues to be lovingly cherished and greatly appreciated at Balavil. Glaucoma forced the Whites to retire and move into a railway cottage, greatly helped by the intervention of our local M.P. Sir Russell Johnstone, who cut through red tape as though it were butter.

Robbie Gair's sister, Joyce and her husband, then a manciple (janitor) at Glenalmond School had started using the vacant flat during the school holidays and helping at our busy times. Her mother's illness, and the loss of a daughter killed whilst standing at a bus-stop on the eve of her wedding, brought back a desire to live in the valley, and they moved in permanently. It has been a long and happy partnership. We have all benefitted greatly from their country lore and wisdom, and Balavil has flowers inside and out, as though we had moved to Devon. We are 1,000 feet above sea level and on the fifty ninth parallel, so it truly was Joyce's miracle.

Duncan joined Ishbel riding, but as this phase passed he skied, stalked, fished or walked the hills. I replaced horses with two Highland cows, one red, the other black, eleven St. Kilda sheep and some Soays, plus hens and ducks. The bulling and the tupping became a very serious topic, but the former was resolved by Alex Anderson, the cattleman at Rothiemurchus, undertaking the onerous task of transportation with Johnny Grant's trailer, and the neighbouring Wild Life Park supplied the five-horned woolly St. Kilda's tup for some years, now replaced by the equally horny male from Hugh Earl of Cawdor at the renowned castle of Shakespeare's MacBeth. The demise of the Wild Life Park's tup bears recounting. We had a very severe winter when even the fast-flowing Spey was frozen with ice so thick that we were able to drive the Landrover across it. One morning I looked out at first light which comes to us after nine o'clock in midwinter and saw the black tup standing rigid, frozen like a statue. Duncan and I bundled it into the Landrover, and he sat in the back pushing its forelegs back and forward to restore circulation as his father did to his arms when he was cold. We got to the vet and the tup survived, but his fertility had gone forever. The vet said solemnly "Let that be a lesson to you, never to make love in the garden in thirty five degrees of frost".

George Rafferty, the famous T.V. Vet from Grantown, was the expert who looked after the animals. One year he maintained we had a spectacular black bull calf, so we registered our first pedigree bull Tom Macdhu Macpherson 1st of Balavil. He failed his early fertility test but hope springs eternal and he is now reported sound. After all his namesake was a late starter! He was thirty three years old when we married.

In 1976 when Duncan was five years old, I received a letter from the Reverend Dr. Fraser McLuskey, minister of St. Columba's, who had christened him. As well as Princess Grace, Duncan had some of my dearest friends as godparents – Sarah Redesdale, Dr. Rob Kennedy, and of the younger generation Charles Fforde from Arran, and they have all supported him splendidly. Dr. McLuskey's letter invited me to join the eldership of the Church.

There are many women Elders in Scotland but they had not yet broken the ranks of this very big Central London Church of St. Columba. I took the letter up to my mother-in-law, Lady Macpherson, who was within one month of her one hundredth and first birthday. She read it with very great care. She got out her magnifying glass and read it again. She had been in bed with a flu bug for several days. After tea I was busy writing in my room when she asked for me to go through and see her again. She greeted me with the words "Jean. you do not mean you are going to be an Elder of the Scottish Church, you mean my seventh, my darling Tommy, my youngest son will be put forward for the Eldership." "No! No!" I said. "You can see quite clearly in the letter it is me. I do not think that Tommy would have the time". She replied "I do not approve, not in any way. Jean, you have not given your life to one single service like a nurse, a teacher to the handicapped, the Red Cross or N.S.P.C.C. – I most definitely do not approve." She died the next day.

Her resting place was in Newtonmore Cemetery, and the service took place in the village. We had most of her direct descendants, who numbered forty-six and the next of kin in for lunch at Balavil. It was a cold March day, we collected some very tired and frozen heather and tied it up into a great big wreath. I had put a card on it from "All the Tommy Macphersons". After lunch we had a family photograph and in the usual breathless rush we all piled into the cars. Suddenly I realised that the wreath at the back had not one but two cards. Duncan had helped me make our card. He had used a coat hanger hook to secure not just my card but another on which he had roughly printed "Dear God look after Granny. She was a good woman".

Hill House had Duncan until he asked, aged eight, why he could not go away like his friends. So to the Dragon School at Oxford, he went, where he reported on his first week-end there "the food is much better than at home and I can talk all night with boys in my bedroom and wake up and swim, and use the carpentry room". How could a mother compete? He has gone on to Eton and Oxford, has a love of rugby and athletics, like his father, and is now a pupil barrister member of the Middle Temple, having taken a good law degree.

Like his brother and sister, he opted for foreign travel between school and university. As third in line it was difficult to be original, but he managed. He got himself signed on as a supernumerary hand in a container vessel sailing from Tilbury to Mombasa, calling at eight or nine fascinating ports on the way. A spell with friends and a brief job in Kenya, then visiting all the countries southward in East Africa to Zimbabwe where he had a happy time in the hospitable home of Ian and Eileen Henderson. Then on as a freelance co-driver the eight hundred miles to Johannesburg where other welcoming friends like Gavin Relly of Anglo-American had arranged jobs for him. His tasks varied from organising a gang of pig-keepers to being part of a soil-sampling team in the vineyards. A final fling with his father's Oxford rugger friends in Cape Province, then home to University.

He was lucky to have another spare long vacation between Oxford and Bar School, and this time he went by bus or hitchhike through Turkey, Kurdistan, Syria, Lebanon, Jordan, Jerusalem, Petra and Egypt, all on about 200 dollars!

We bought a freehold house in 1980 at 28 Albion Street which backed onto the school as the lease of Somers Crescent was declining. It was a tall thin house and freehold, my husband had had enough of leasehold problems. Our beloved housekeeper Margaret Hemsley and her husband moved in to the basement there, her daughter having married from Somers Crescent and left home. We had put in a new heating system, re-wired the house, built a room at the back which moved the garden up a level. My husband reluctantly realised that we were stuck with two houses in London. Somers Crescent was large and the slump of the early eighties was a quiet time for house sales. One evening he had gone over to 28 Albion Street, and at the gates two of the Hyde Park School parents were admiring this particular house. My husband persuaded them to bid against each other to see how much they would pay for the house and then undertook to consider the higher offer. He telephoned me at Balavil to say he was taking me out to dinner by myself, to celebrate the sale of the house. I returned south immediately, to learn that it was the Albion Street house he had sold. I was amazed and asked that, if we were going to remain at Somers Crescent it had to be for at least a further five years. He agreed. At that moment my twin sister and her husband entered the local restaurant and said that I had promised that should our finances be over-stretched, we would sell it to them. Fortunately this was possible and my sister and her family live in the house to this day. My mother has a flat in it and it has proved to be a very happy home. Margaret Hemsley patiently moved back to Somers Crescent with us.

My twin sister, Anne, has of course been important in my life. She has a strong personality, natural leadership and was academically gifted. These qualities first became evident during our war years together. At the outbreak of the 1939-45 war Anne and I were evacuated to Canada via Liverpool docks to Montreal on the s.s. Duchess of Bedford. The three week journey across the Atlantic was cold and crowded. Mrs. Margaret Gardner-Medwin, a Canadian married to the distinguished Liverpool Professor of Architecture, was returning home with David and Andrew, aged four years and eighteen months and was our guardian. Lights were not permitted and food was strictly rationed. Anne ensured that we all got our fair share and on one occasion an orange rolled down the steep staircase aided by the high waves from the storm outside and disappeared down the corridor under the skirt of a passing nun. Like lightning it was retrieved by Anne with a quick wiggle between the holy legs only to find her guardian on the other side! To avoid enemy ships we passed beside Newfoundland where there were enormous icebergs sailing by, one with a polar bear on it. This was the last time children crossed the Atlantic as her sister ship s.s. Duchess of Atholl went down three weeks later with no life saved.

We lived in Toronto with Margaret Gardner-Medwin's sister, Mrs. Kay Campbell, the gifted musician wife of Dr. Donald Campbell, who mastered my troublesome lungs so well that together Anne and I could start at St. Clement's School for Girls in Toronto. Sound scholastic studies greatly helped us to upgrade the mis-mash of education in Broomfield House, Didsbury, then in Switzerland, then a governess. The dry air of snow, and sun and holiday fun at

Camp Oconto with the quiet happy life of our guardian gave me a love for Canada, its people and its way of life which I will always try to emulate. Anne was always my protector, buying bus tickets or spending pocket money. Our eventual journey home unscathed in Spring 1944 found us awaiting a ship out of Philadelphia as the guests of the great Miss Packard, of motor car fame. The glittering, exciting life continued when weeks later the s.s. Serpa Pinta undertook to transport us to Portugal. It was a carefree time, with an older friend, the distinguished skier, Sheena Mackintosh, aboard with us. Now she is Mrs. Ruaraidh Hilleary, a great equestrian expert, living not too far away at Logie Farm, by Forres.

Music and bright lights on this neutral vessel made sure no submarine would attack us. The only sign of war was Portuguese soldiers coming on board in the Azores and sleeping on deck. On arrival as the guests of the government we stayed in Estoril, near Lisbon and visited a lace-making convent and the Casino. At thirteen this made exciting living, but Anne filled in all the right forms and soon we were off to Southern Ireland flying in an old fat sea-plane. It was colder and quieter at the Convent of the Sacred Heart in Limerick and the three day wait filled me with fear and with wheezes. Apart for a few days between my schooling in Switzerland and a governess class in Sidford, Devon, I had not seen my parents for seven years and I was fourteen inches taller.

The final flight to London brought us to an Army base and children were met by their families in a large deserted hangar. When everyone else had gone, an official came from the office and said "You must be the Butler-Wilson twins. Your parents are at your elder sister's confirmation at Hawnes School, Haynes Park, Bedfordshire, and we are to put you on a train there". Hungry and dejected we followed. What an awful decision our parents had had to make – I expect that they had been given many dates for our arrival. After further delays, late in the evening the train brought us to the railway station rendezvous. No very tall Daddy and Mummy greeted us, and a couple waiting stood and watched as we walked back and forth. When clearly no-one else was going to emerge, Anne went over. We had not recognised our parents.

Lice and fleas and chicken pox kept us away from the Hawnes School. When these had been sorted out, we returned to 25 Sandeleigh Avenue to the very bed I had left so long ago. Edith, our Nanny, was there to greet us. I had remembered her and the long-spouted brass kettle that again was busy in front of the open fire giving my lungs an inhalation. Old Dr. Grant Davy recommended leaving the River Mersey – and poor father had to go to the expense of a move to Alderley Edge in Cheshire. There we attended St. Hilary's Church of England Day School, and then together as boarders to Acton Reynold School near Shrewsbury. I shared my room with Nicola Cayzer. She put up with my wheezes and I with her emotional tears. We were a solace to each other, and we are both able now to look comfortably back, and laugh.

In 1955 my twin sister, Anne, married Terence Stuart Mallinson, my husband's boss's youngest son. As a student she had joined me at the Edinburgh College of Domestic Science, now Queen Margaret's College in the University. She participated fully in the sporting and academic life there. After leaving college she had the opportunity to return to Canada when the Commonwealth Games Team went to British Columbia. Then she became the Community Relations Officer for the American Air Force in Essex and it was here that the Mallinsons had their home, a Lutyens house in Woodford. This gave Anne the opportunity to be based near her fiancé.

After her marriage she became a Justice of the Peace and the first lay magistrate to sit with the Lord Mayor of London at his Mansion House Court, the first woman on the Marlborough School Council, and became together with Shirley Porter, a Councillor for the Hyde Park Ward of the Westminster City Council. In 1986 she was Lord Mayor of Westminster, the first married lady in that office; so her husband became the first Consort. Anne was one of the few ladies on the Council of St. Mary's Medical School and continued when it united with Imperial College and Chairman of the Tower Hamlets Health Board and of the

Montessori St. Nicholas Centre, which is the only one in Britain founded by Dr. Maria Montessori. She raised the sum of one million pounds for Beauchamp Lodge Settlement, and founded a Home Safety Charity of which the Duchess of Gloucester is the Patron, and with her passion for the environment she plants trees wherever practicable in the City of Westminster. Like the proverbial fairy she and her family live literally at the bottom of the garden.

By 1982 Chesterton's had more or less given up hope of getting a through road or a mews in the Long Garden, as the whole of Connaught Street and Archery Close had become a conservation area. John Hollamby, who had always made it clear to the Church Commissioners that the School was a tremendous asset to their Estate, then came to me and offered instead of our annual licence a ninety-nine year lease of the Long Garden to me for £25,000, so that we could really plan ahead. The mills of the Church Commissioners do not grind speedily, and it was not until 1987 that they finalised their paper work. By that time Chesterton's management had changed and they did not honour their £25,000 offer which we had accepted in 1982, but imposed a new price of £50,000. This hugely added to our fund-raising problems but we had to agree.

I got a letter asking me to call at Number 1 Millbank and sign the ninety-nine year lease. That morning I looked outside and saw it was raining, I put on a waterproof coat and a pair of wellington boots, and with my Shetland dogs, Shamus and his mother Morag, walked across Hyde Park, Green Park, St. James's Park and then round the corner to Number 1 Millbank. It is a very awe-inspiring building with huge doors and, inside, black and white diced marble floors. Before I could set foot inside the Commissionaire said "You cannot come in here like that, soaking wet, and with two wet dogs". I fumbled around with my zips and found the letter which confirmed my twelve noon appointment. The Commissionaire took me in to the beautiful elegant hall and telephoned to let them know that I had arrived. A charming gentleman came down by lift and told me that a lunch had been laid on for me and would I like to come upstairs.

I explained that I had come with dogs and could not come up in my muddy boots or my stockinged feet. I thanked him and declined lunch. I signed the documents behind the lift on the ground floor and then walked happily home with my dogs.

# CHAPTER FIVE

The school had for some time been a limited company for administrative convenience. My husband and I were the shareholders, but there were no dividends paid and no salaries drawn by us. The surplus from the fees was used to help children in need – generally children whose parents had already paid fees previously and suffered some sad piece of family misfortune, such as death or severe illness; or financial calamity, a messy divorce or even abandonment, which is particularly common in the case of unmarried mothers.

When under pressure to expand we undertook the huge task of the Long Garden and the new buildings, and with all the attendant capital cost it was clear that external finance was needed. We had no wish to follow the road of turning the School into a commercial proposition and squeezing profits from it, as opposed to treating it as a vocation and a pre-school ideal. So in 1977 we took counsel of the Charity Commissioners, and with their help created the Hyde Park Nursery School Charitable Fund (Reg No 275748).

The first trustees were my husband, who has always been deeply involved with my activities, together with Mrs. Gerald Ellison, Lady Sherfield and Lady Read. Jane Ellison, as I have already said, was the wife of the very distinguished Bishop of London who had helped in the early stages. From the start she had been very interested in the School, our high standards and our aims. We had known the Ellisons since his days as Bishop of Chelmsford in which diocese lived at that time one of my sisters-in-law, and Jane remained a trustee until their departure from London on retirement. Alice Sherfield was a very industrious person, of great administrative competence, and an active and helpful trustee. My husband had known Lord Sherfield as Head of the Foreign Office and as a distinguished ambassador, and much later in his role as Chairman of the glamorous Wells Fargo Bank, a direct descendant from the American wild west.

Alice came into my life when they took occupation of a garage next to ours, at the back of our Somers Crescent home, and we became firm friends. Sadly ill health after a decade forced her to give up external activities and she died shortly afterwards. The other trustee from the beginning was Lady Read, wife of Sir John Read. They were also in Somers Crescent, and at that time he was Chairman of E.M.I. Later he was Chairman of the T.S.B. at the time of its slightly controversial flotation. At the same time my husband was a Director of T.S.B. Scotland. Dorothy Read was another extremely efficient person with a deep and loving commitment to charitable work that would do real and visible good to people whose need you could personally see. She gave us a great deal of help and guidance, but her main activity was for the blind in Loughton. One of their occupational activities was basket work of excellent quality and we became customers. At that time we had five dogs – two black labradors in Scotland and three Shetland sheep dogs that travelled everywhere with me, and we must have acquired some twenty splendid dog baskets so that they knew their place in every room! The Reads moved out of town to Hove, so reluctantly we bade farewell to Dorothy as a trustee.

The successors to the first trustees are Mrs. George Martin and Lady Redesdale and no charity could have a better team. Judy Martin and her husband came to live opposite us in No. 5 Somers Crescent, one of the new houses, and we did a lot together. Their son Giles is a contemporary of Duncan and he now has his own pop group. George Martin is one of the country's most prominent figures in the world of modern music. He played a big part in the building of the Beatles in the sixties, that phenomenon of Liverpool sound which added a new dimension to the global scene. When they left London for their beautiful country house in Wiltshire, they also established a recording studio of major importance on the West Indian island of Montserrat. George says that getting the pop stars to come there is well worth the cost, as once there, they are totally under control, not the case in London!

As an aside, we have been very fortunate in our neighbours. The Martins sold their house to Sir Peter Graham, then Chairman of Standard Chartered Bank, and he and his elegant wife Lyn became good friends. I have already written about our American neighbours, and particularly the Beales. Tom Beale was the Economic Counsellor at the U.S. Embassy in London, and became Ambassador in Jamaica. With Rita I had visited Russia and the United States, and I also went to stay with them in Jamaica. My means of travel was on a Tate and Lyle sugar boat, by courtesy of Tommy's cousin, Peter Runge, who was then the Chairman. One of the nicest men, Peter was very able and when President had created the Confederation of British Industries by merging the previous Federation of British Industries with the National Union of Manufacturers, to make a concentrated lobby for business. In that context he started my husband's involvement in the politics of business by encouraging him to stand for election to the C.B.I.'s London and South East Regional Council, of which he shortly became Chairman. I have never known whether to be grateful or not. It has clearly been an absorbing interest, but also absorbing of time of which I have not willingly ceded.

Peter was doubly connected with us. He married Tommy's first cousin Fiona Macpherson, sister of David Strathcarron, and Peter's sister married Tommy's brother, Niall, Lord Drumalbyn. Niall was one of the last created hereditary peers. Sadly he had no male heir, but two splendid daughters carry on his line, Mary a distinguished barrister in the complex section of planning laws and Jean, who is married to Vice-Admiral Sir James Weatherall R.N. (Rtd), newly installed in St. James's Palace as Marshal of the Diplomatic Corps. It really slays me to be the aunt, even by marriage, to a retired admiral!

So Peter arranged my trip provided I had a lady companion, as we would be the only passengers. My dear friend, Jean Fforde from Arran had a brother, Lord Ronald Graham, in Jamaica and she readily agreed to come with me. We boarded the 7,000 ton vessel, shaped rather like a small oil tanker, at Tilbury with all the excitement that dockside and family send-offs generate. The weather forecast was awful and the ship, returning empty to fetch sugar, had not had time to take on its normal load of ballast. We left the sheltered waters of the Thames and the Channel, and soon faced heavy seas. On the first morning, the steward brought tea on a tray to Jean's bedside, lost his balance and shed the contents of the scalding pot onto her hip and behind. The Captain immediately said he was in charge of medical matters on board and would anoint the affected area with the appropriate remedy, but Jean who is Junoesque in build and, when she wishes, formidable in manner, told him in no uncertain terms to think again. So I spent the first sea-faring days regularly applying anti-burn ointment to milady's rear! We had to heave to for a day or two off the Azores, and took no less than twenty one days to reach Jamaica, but we are both good sailors and had a lot of fun.

Other neighbours in our street whom we saw a lot were the Le Marchants and the Browns. Spencer and Cindy Le Marchant were directly opposite for many years, with lovely and lively girls, Geva and Peronel. Cindy was, I believe, the daughter of the Mr. Simpson whose subsequent wife Wallis, caused such a constitutional crisis in the brief reign of Edward VIII. Spencer, an eminent stock-broker, became M.P. for High Peak, and very popular in the House of Commons and the constituency, until his sadly early death.

The Browns were American, one of the first families to move into the new houses when the street was largely rebuilt. Nicholas, a U.S. Navy Officer and Naval Attaché at the Embassy in Grosvenor Square, was of the family that founded Brown University, one of the Ivy League group. Diane his lovely wife, is French, and they both shared my husband's interest in good wine. He is now in retirement and in charge of what I am told is the world's largest maritime museum in Baltimore, while keeping up, in Virginia, his British habit of hunting, pink coat and all. We keep in close touch with them. Their daughter, on honeymoon, stayed with us in Scotland and we enjoyed their son David's wedding in Boston.

Lady Redesdale is a natural as a trustee because she had been involved from the start. Sarah has inexhaustible energy and is a born organiser. Her advice has guided me, her drive has spurred me on, and her sympathy has comforted me time after time over the years. Ishbel is closest to Tessa Mitford of all Sarah's daughters, but we know and love them all. Clem, her husband, working for Chase Bank and busy in the House of Lords, shared a bond with me in our common tendency to asthma. Sadly he died last year. His son Rupert, my good looking godson, is today the youngest active peer in the House of Lords and winning golden opinions. Sarah copes brilliantly with her large family and three houses. She is, and I hope will continue to be, a tower of strength to us all.

When I gave up all connections with the School, except as a consultant to Ravenstone House, it was felt proper for me to become a trustee. Previously, as principal, it had been deemed that there might be the possibility of conflict of interest. So I was appointed a trustee in 1992, and we await the confirmation of the Charity Commission which apparently takes time.

It is, I think, worth recounting quite fully what the Charitable Fund was aiming to do, directly and through the Hyde Park School. The objective was to raise funds for the capital expenditure needed properly to care for one hundred very young children, and for the annual continuous revenue expenditure to support some 15% of free or aided children. But why run the school at all? What was so special about it?

In 1989 we were encouraged to submit a nomination for the School for the prestigious Jerwood Award for educational innovation. The trustees drew up a comprehensive statement which expresses our purposes so I reproduce it in full:

*Jerwood Award*
*Nomination of Hyde Park School*

*Introduction*
    The Charitable Fund, which owns but does not manage the Hyde Park School, has noted the interest that the Jerwood Foundation has expressed in original contributions to the theory and practice of education.

We have no doubt that the assessors may have initially in mind the major areas of secondary and subsequent education.

We submit however that pre-school education is an area of increasing public concern and importance, and that it is now widely accepted that correct handling of the education aspects of the very early years has a significant effect on character equilibrium and on ability to learn throughout the remainder of an educational career.

We therefore submit what we believe are the very real innovative contributions of the Hyde Park School for consideration in regard to the Jerwood Award. We would summarise these as follows:

a) The education of children at a young age of widely different backgrounds, some able to pay fees and some not, without any child or parent knowing whether any other is fee paying, aided or free.

b) The establishment of a charity which enables the fee paying surplus to provide for the aided and free children.

c) The underlying belief that stability, continuity and normality are the essentials for children, particularly for those whose home life gives any cause for concern.

d) The availability of high quality teaching so that children have a flying start at primary school with an already acquired knowledge of numbers and letters, combined with an accessibility of the school's facilities from 8.30 a.m. to 6.00 p.m. every weekday of the year, even outside school terms, to deal with emergency situations which arise in both ordered and disordered households.

The demand upon the school appears inexhaustible and meeting it is limited only by financial considerations.

*Reasons for Pre-School Care*

It is well known that the social requirement of nursery schools has been given a high profile in recent times. The increase in employment of married women, the social acceptance of a working career for the young mother and the economic need for family input into the national workforce are all manifest considerations. The provision of facilities by the State or by local authorities is inadequate in total and in most cases grossly inadequate in quality, amounting to the barest minimum of childminding supervision. Given the need, locally and nationally, to upgrade the situation, particularly by provision in the private sector, it is worth examining the merits respectively of the school or the playgroup approach. Both, if well run with a high

**HYDE PARK NURSERY SCHOOL – JUNE 1981**

*Back Row:* Miss Sally Dean, James Bussell, Felicity Anderson-Lyne, Nicholas Johnson, Nicola Marcel, Stuart Rowe.

*5th Row:* Mrs. Kay Munro, Miss Debbie Sanders, Aisha Mckenzie, Tariq Al-Khater, Natalie Kadas, Danielle Crompton, Milan Corcoran, Claudia Massey, Miss Margaret Greaves, Mrs. Ann Saunders, Mrs. Molly Piper.

*4th Row:* Christina Ritter, Morad Salmanpour, Dimitris Efthymiou, Nicholas Ginsberg, Simon Vasco, Sebastian Chander, Joshua Gray, Emile Khadder, Shayman Al-Mashat, Naser Yasin-Deimezis, Fiesal Gaderi, Daniel Weston, Richard Price, Nicholas Singh, Yusef El-Ansari.

*3rd Row:* Angus Hilleary, Rupert Willats, Katie Roth, Harley McKinley, Alina Polemis, David Brim, Alexandra Townsley, Stefan Hanania, Ross Lockhart, Hamid Amirani.

*2nd Row:* Talal Khawaja, Thomas Norcliffe, Lee Mohlere, Alexander Cain, Leisha Brace, Pascal Yefet, William Mills, Louise Sorensen.

*Front Row:* Amna Ghani, Iman El-Gharib, Nikolas Halper, Melanie Weston, Claire Glorney, Jenny Kay, Toby Miller, Annemarie Gorman, Tarun Buxani, Poppy Edwards, Nasser Al-Ka'abi.

**HYDE PARK NURSERY SCHOOL – 1982**

*Back Row:* Miss Margaret Greaves, Mrs. Ann Keating, Miss Sally Dean, Nicholas Ginsberg, Jenny Kaye, Thomas Norcliffe, Miss Caroline Garrard, Miss Debbie Sanders, Mrs. Kay Munro.

*4th Row:* Jack Hussein, Helene Skinas, Nicolas Singh, Danielle Crompton, Katie Roth, Bettina Davidson, Frances Moffatt, Laura Gibson, Yusuf El Ansari, Alina Polemis, Melanie Weston, Michael Brim, Zaylie Bussell.

*3rd Row:* Elizabeth Hanniffy, Titi Ademolu, Seraj Darak, Iman El-Gharib, Jacques Schooler, Zainab Shehu-Awak, Ross Lockhart, Leisha Brace, Nikolas Halper, Lee Mohlere, Alexander Cain, Ateh Damachi, Aymeric Bucher, Victoria Stone, Jonathan Harvey, Sara Jameel, Kimberly Morgan.

*2nd Row:* Jane Warwick, Poppy Edwards, Serena Mattar, Beth Button, Yaomina Asseily, Dina Andreadis, Gabrielle Tarant, Fiona Cameron, Daphne Valambous, Annemarie Gorman, Rebecca Wade, Richard Gibson.

*Front Row:* Davinia Cheetham-Salik, Gayatri Punj, Kayvan Salmanpour, Sasha Brenner, Georgina Townsley, Lorenzo Cenci Di Bello, Bibi Lemos, Kim Harris, Claire Glorney,

**HYDE PARK NURSERY SCHOOL – 1983**

*Back Row:* Mrs. Kay Munro, Mrs. Ann Keating, Miss Sally Dean, Bibi Lemos, Petronella Gordon-Dean, Zaylie Bussell, Michael Brim, Daphne Valambous, Miss Debbie Sanders, Miss Margaret Greaves, Joel Gazdar.

*5th Row:* Lorenzo Cenci, Frances Moffatt, Kayvan Salmanpour, Serena Mattar, Victoria Stone, Yasmina Asseily, Dina Andreadis, Alina Polemis, Fiona Beaton.

*4th Row:* Leon Polemis, Davinia Cheetham-Salik, Gideon Nedas, Gabrielle Tarant, Turget Guneri, Miranda Hafez, Gian Paul Becci, Rebecca Maxwell, Sam Dymond, Zahra Siddiqui, Ali Malik, Kim Harris.

*3rd Row:* Aysem Monaco, Claire Glorney, Tori Cardoso, Anseiy Ali, Mustafa Khalili, Jarene Theinissen, Rajiv Bajaria, Daisy Le Vay, Faisal Alauddin, Richard Powell, Nora Badr, Nofel Al-Abdulaly, Nancy Fahmy, Oliver Glass, Mariam Polding.

*2nd Row:* Melanie Weston, Georgina Townsley, Stavros Livanos, Louise Butler, Rebecca Wade, Edward Watts, Catherine Foroughi, Natalie Lockton, Michael Zolotos, Victoria Burton, Richard Gibson, Samina Virani, Vishal Melwani, Safinaz El-Ansari, Hisham Hasan.

*Front Row:* Philomena Keat, Adham El-Gharib, Saifal Alauddin, Sasha Brenner, Aaron Merali, Jeanne Hancock, Benjamin Howard, Vivienne Criaz, Comert Guneri, Joanne Moffatt, Gabriel Markson, Maria Porfyratos, Adam Khorshid, Diana Koostra, Yannis Valambous.

## HYDE PARK SCHOOL– 1984

*Back Row:* Maria Porfryratos, Marianna Trechakis, Benjamin Linnit, Zaylie Bussell, Georgina Townsley.

*6th Row:* Miss Nikki Frizell. Tori Cardoso, Lloyd Turner, Nora Badr, James Britton, Richard Powell, Leonidas Polemis, Miss Sally Dean.

*5th Row:* Miss Judith Sommervill, Oliver Glass, Diana Kootstra, Joel Gazdar, James Jenkins, Aaron Merali, Vishal Melwani, Naime Ismail, Richard Gibson, Mrs. Ann Keating.

*4th Row:* Karim Sultan, Sasha Brenner, Gabriel Markson, Natalie Lockton, Yannis Valambous, Sharon Tan, Miss Debbie Sanders.

*3rd Row:* Nofel Abdulaly, Joanna Preston, Steven Garcia, Sam Dymond, Jeanne Hancock, Kern Schmid, Virginia Frasure, Edward Watts, Stavros Livanos, Rebecca Wade, Saiful Alauddin, Daisy Le Vay, Philomena Keet, Kayvan Salmanpour, Christopher Webley.

*2nd Row:* Jemima Key, Sara Davies, Zahra Siddiqui, Alexandra Versariu, Sulafah Jabari, Veronica Vasco, Victoria Burton, Safinaz El-Ansari, Jo-Jo-Jackson, Joanne Moffatt, Rebecca Maxwell.

*Front Row:* Marc Munro, Camilla Noble-Warren, Hosni Diarra, Katie Glass, Sameer Dalamal, Philippa Soskin, Gorgie Tziras, Danai Murewa, Joshua Lehmann, Dana Al Kuroshi, Alexander Redfern.

## HYDE PARK SCHOOL – 1985

*Back Row:* Miss Beth Wareham, Miss Teresa Roche, Miss Sally Dean, Philip Moore, Lloyd Turner, Joanne Moffett, James Jenkins, Joanna Preston, Matthew McFarlane, Nofel Al-Abulaly, Mrs. Kay Munro, Miss Sue Richards, Miss Debbie Sanders.

*4th Row:* Karen Lawee, Alexander Redfern, Marianna Tzoumaras, Marc Munro, Dana Al-Toubi, Marc Sodhy, Marianna Trechakis, Cy Elliott Smith, Danai Murerwa, Kem Schmid, Sulafah Jabarti, Adham El-Gharib, Charlotte Parker.

*3rd Row:* Safinaz El-Ansari, Aaron Merali, Naime Ismail, Karin Sultan, Yumma Saleh, Eddy Albasry, Hala Moawad, Drew Conroy, Maria Porfryratos, Georgie Tziras, Jemima Key, Luke Archer Nolan.

*2nd Row:* Abbas Lalljee, Anthony Whitehead, Tanya Israni, Joshua Lehmann, Camilla Noble-Warren, Troy Potter, Dima Nawbar, Nasr Hamood, Kadija Shai, James Theinissen, Angela Lemos, Alastair Rowe, Camilla Bates.

*Front Row:* Edward Balfour, Gautam Khanna, Kriston Andon, Jade Hope, Ramsey Mahmoud, Tebecca Miller, Walid Khalili, Lamia Moawad, Harry Key, Insha Rizva, James Harris, James Elderton.

## HYDE PARK SCHOOL – 1986

*Back Row:* Mrs. Ann Saunders, Miss Beth Wareham, Miss Alice Colman, Insha Rizvi, Dana Al-Kutoubi, James Harris, Camilla Noble-Warren, Joshua Lehmann, Dima Newbar, Hebet Yousuf, Miss Kay Evans, Miss Sue Richards, Mrs. Kay Munro.

*4th Row:* Alexander Sage, Karin Irani, Elliot Schmid, Camilla Bates, Henry Embleton, Katherine Hardy, Alexander Delmont, Asselah Hamood, Humza Siddiqui, Stephanie Mashor, Habby Zhainidi, Dyala Roda, Alistair Rowe, Kimi Takibashai.

*3rd Row:* Mark MacLeish, Kriston Andon, Sarah Osman, Mona Khan, Nasr Hamood, Ramsey Mahmoud, Farah Hameed, Wael Irani, Kadiji Shai, Marc Munro, Rafezah Abdul Rahman, Drew Conroy, Jade Hope, Chester Chipperfield, Vanessa Wozniak, Shakthi Vijayakumar.

*2nd Row:* Eddy Albasry, Yasmin Albasry, James Thaunissen, Moneaza Siddiqui, Cy Elliot Smith, Maarya Saidi, Anthony Whitehead, Carly Runcorn, Abbas Lalljee, Tanya Israni, Max Lehmann.

*Front Row:* Tariq Fancy, Mark Manduca, Hafidz Yusof, Juan Carlos Arroya, Jonathan Miller, Simba Murerwa, Ashleigh Tanner, Tania Newbar, Timothy Whitehead, Edward Brauns, Salam Rassi, Nichol Talreia, Charles Jenkins, Elves Gabel, Rufus Gordon-Dean.

## HYDE PARK SCHOOL – SUMMER 1987

*Back Row:* Miss Sue Richards, Miss Beth Wareham, Mrs. Kay Munro, Henry Embleton, Natasha Kilby, Habby Zainidi, Rufus Gordon-Dean, Ashleigh Tanner, Chester Chipperfield, Danny Shashou, Sabrina Currumbhoy, Alexander Baird, Miss Kay Evans, Miss Caroline Barlow, Miss Harriet Smallwood.

*4th Row:* Dina Amin, Alexander Burton, Gadah Al Abdulaly, Nadir Al Jabry, Alexander Valdes, Mark MacLeish, Vanessa Wozniak, Elliott Schmid, Insha Rizvi.

*3rd Row:* Assam Al Raisi, Hind Habih, Alastair Jessop, Sameer Yousuf, Alastair Rowe, Salam Rassi, Harith Al Anbari, Nichol Talreja, Sean Rajanayaka, Joan Carlos Arroyo, Max Lehmann, Timothy Whitehead, Sherrif Osman, Gavin Tucker, Faizen Siddiqi, Timothy Tomkinson.

*2nd Row:* Panchesta Braune, Tanua Sodhy, Sara Amin, Laura Dowsett, Tanya Nawbar, Rowanna Kong, Annabelle Le Havre, Lucy Edwards, Alexia Dhruve, Ranwa Obeid, Shakthi Vijayakumar, Monica Larkin, Katie Simpson.

*Front Row:* Adam Butterfield, Oscar Duffy, Charles Jenkins, Daniel Harris, Kimberley Salmon, Celine Redfern, Emma Davies, Edward Braune, Omar Khan, Basil Kronfli, Xavier Amon-Tanoh.

**HYDE PARK SCHOOL – 1988**

*Back Row:* Miss Sue Richards, Miss Caroline Barlow, Miss Alice Fleetwood, Miss Kay Evans, Miss Alice Colman, Miss Harriett Smallwood.

*5th Row:* Oscar Duffy, Sherif Osman, Hafidz Yusof, Alistair Jessop, Sarko Kalaydiian, Enrico Cividino, James Profumo, Mark MacLeish, Kimi Takebayashi, Edward Braune, Abdul Al Alawi.

*4th Row:* Mrs. Ann Saunders, Nina Kaneko, Celine Redfern, Maryam Al-Subaie, Sarah Sreih, Roanna Kong, Monica Larkin, Annabellee e Harve, Ranwa Obeid, Hind Habib, Nihal Salah, Anna Hussin, Jamila Brown, Timmy Whitehead, Mrs. Kay Munro.

*3rd Row:* Waleed Al-Alawi, Rami Khatib, Basil Kronfli, Alexander Burton, Daniel Harris, Haitham Al-Aboulay, Stephen Michelini, Jack Powell, Robertino Habib, Tariq Al-Jabry, Fahd Al-Rashid, Sara Jaber, Adam Butterfield, Sara Amin.

*2nd Row:* Kimberley Salmon, Soraya Bahrami, Emma Davies, Fay Robinson, Panchita Braune, Charlotte Radcliffe, Rachel Simm, Melissa Mally, Fadia Al-Malazi, Corolina Roja.

*Front Row:* Robert Argent, Elizabeth Jenkins, Cedrych Chan, Alexandria Lemos, Jonathan Dean, Vishesh Shah, Edward Saatchi.

staff ratio, will give the introduction to community life which forms a sound basis for the future and is particularly significant in small family situations. It can however be maintained that the unstructured activities of the playgroup do not achieve the gentle approach to discipline and self-discipline which is beneficially absorbed at that age, but may later come as a shock which can even provoke resentment. It is also widely argued by professionals that early co-ordination by hand and eye which leads quite easily on to focusing on letters and numbers gives an educational lead which is not subsequently lost.

However, the concentration span of the very young is limited. Rest, variety, music and movement, and outdoor play must all be included. The conclusion of the founder of Hyde Park School, some twenty six years ago, was that the two systems, school and playgroup, should be combined in twin form. First the school, with its teaching discipline and structured pattern, should be within the children's capacity, with hours depending on age group and with a broadly standard term time and holiday time calendar. It should be for those children where the family circumstances can ensure regular and continuous attendance over a period which allows the child to settle down and feel this is a normal way of life. Second, the playgroup aspect should take place after the children's learning capacity is fulfilled during term-time, and all day during the holidays, both for regular attenders and for those whose attendance is spasmodic or even from time to time unique, because of family circumstances. It is interesting to note that this requirement is to a degree in substitution for the leisured maiden aunts of an earlier generation who simply are no longer there.

*Objective*

The school's objective is the very highest possible quality standard of care and instruction for children, and to provide (as a supplement to a normal fee paying structure) free and aided places for children in the catchment area where appropriate circumstances exist.

*Philosophy*

The school's philosophy is that children benefit enormously from regularity, continuity, tranquillity and normality in an orderly routine. The school believes that children on their own have no class or race consciousness and that their exposure to social mixtures at an early age is thoroughly beneficial, provided any question of financial status remains, as is the school's principle, on a basis of complete anonymity.

The free and aided children come from Churches of the area, social services recommendation, St. Mary's Hospital and the Sick Children's Hospital, advertisements, and particularly by word of mouth. Because of inevitable financial limitations, the school cannot seek to absorb the whole area of absolute poverty. While candidates are certainly accepted if they come from such an area, the main thrust is when a family breakdown occurs through relative poverty, that is to say a very sharp negative change of circumstances for which very many internal and external causes have been encountered. There is a strong insistence in all cases that the children should not be just dumped. Teaching and supervision is of course all done by fully qualified staff, but the school also seeks to ensure a strong degree of parental interest in every way that the working parent can spare participation time, as a spectator for various activities and to give an overall feeling to the child of the family involvement.

*Conclusion*

We understand that with the structure of a 52 week a year availability, 5 days a week bar Christmas Day and Good Friday for young children in an educational environment, there is a proper claim that this establishment is unique in London if not in the U.K.

We believe also that in the financial and educational structure indicated above, there have evolved genuine innovative characteristics which are worthy of a submission for the Jerwood Award.

We accordingly submit the name and achievements of the Hyde Park School for your consideration.

We did not win, because the Jerwood terms proved to confine them to later age-groups, but we were highly commended by Dr. Michael Hooker, the assessor who gave us much valuable advice in his previous role with Trumen & Knightley and later from sheer kindness.

As I have written at the beginning of this chapter, the Charitable Fund has supported at Hyde Park School and still supports at its successor, Ravenstone House, Hyde Park, a steady stream of children resident in the locality whose parents, for whatever reasons, cannot meet the normal fees in full. We measure their misfortune as adverse change of circumstances, generally financial, and in today's era of financial uncertainty, of social change, and/or moral laxity there are all too many causes of such a change, generally leaving the innocent parent and the young child as the ones to suffer. It tugs at the heart strings to read the letters of application, the notes of interviews, the detailed statements of the parent's income and severely restrained expenditure, the efforts to earn and to contribute. And it is correspondingly heart-warming to read the letters of appreciation and gratitude, and know of a child's success story created in the aftermath of a personal tragedy.

With the aided children I never considered my task completed when they reached leaving age. I had formed many excellent relationships with schools of different types at the next level, and the records show many successes in achieving entry for these children, where possible with continuing support from new sources.

Meanwhile, going back to the registration of the Hyde Park School Charitable Fund in 1977, my husband and I gave it all the shares of the School's Limited Company, together with an interest free loan of £5,000 and we then set to work to raise funds for the Charity.

I sincerely believe that small local charities, with their almost zero overheads, do the most cost-effective work anywhere, but it is extremely hard to raise money for them against the competition of the famous national organisations.

We found and employed Richard Bird, who was in early retirement, to work for some months largely under my husband's guidance. It was a nail-biting time, because we were expecting the papers from Chestertons on the Long Garden any day, and at their doubled price. We had nothing in the Bank with which to complete the contract.

Gradually, through the generous intervention of friends who influenced various trust funds, money came in. The Astor Foundation, the MacAlpine Foundation, the Grove Charity, the Sassoon Fund, the Englefield Fund, the Ernest Cook Charity, Shell U.K., Robert Fleming, Hill Samuel, Birmid Qualcast, Trafalgar House, Argos and the Metropolitan Police Charity were among our most generous donors.

Our links with the Police dated back to the start of the School. They visited regularly, two at a time, to give little talks on safety and to give the children trust in the Police, sometimes bringing with them the extra excitement of a very docile police horse or a motor bike.

The Baring Foundation made a particularly generous contribution. It was after this, and quite coincidental, that two of my husband's nephews married two Baring sisters!

Our most regularly supportive patrons over the years have been the Esmé Fairbairn Foundation on the capital side, and the Worshipful Company of Dyers and the Charitable Trust of St. George's, Hanover Square on the revenue side for direct support of the aided children term by term.

There is still a desperate need of other regular funds. The need seems to be steadily increasing, often through the bread-winner losing his job mid-way through his family's education, and many more sad cases are brought to me than the present resources can handle.

The original begging letter we sent out had some well-known sponsors, all of whom had children in the School. They included Derek Nimmo, of television fame, and Carl Foreman, the famous film director.

From these patrons developed spontaneously the idea of the "Friends of Hyde Park School", people who shared an affection for the School, enjoyed meeting together, and helped in both fund raising and in social activities. Hilda Chapple, Emily Kronfli, Dr. Ratcliffe, Bonny Dorri, Ann Sim and others. The first summer fair the Briggs lent us a donkey, who patiently walked up the garden and back again all afternoon. The Brims, Schoolers, Willats, Loustau Lalannes, Prestons, Millers, Cromptons, Constantinidis and Wilkins all ran stalls, and a profit of over £2,000 was made. Mrs. Willat's father sold ceramic vases, and the Head Porter of St. Mary's Hospital produced plastic bouquets of flowers to sell. Brian Finlayson, from the St. Columba's congregation, collected items from every corner of London, including a tombola from the D.G.A.A.'s headquarters. To make more time for the "Friends" I had newly retired from the care committee of the Distressed Gentlefolks Aid Association and handed over to Esmé, Viscountess Carlisle.

The inaugural meeting of the Friends was held, organised by Richard Bird during the appeal period, at Somers Crescent in March 1984. It was well attended, and under Mrs. Jean Burton, mother of Victoria and Alexander, as a very active Chairman, she is also a busy hotel-keeper in the district, it went from strength to strength right up to the organising of my final hand-over party when I gave up the management of the School at the end of the Summer term of 1990.

My true love in all my years of work has been the children, but the delightful adults, male and female from the School's little world were an added bonus. Cleaning up the gravestones we came across a broken one, with the initials "J.C." in large letters – all that was left. On one occasion a very traumatised mother came in overwhelmed by some desperate situation in which she was engulfed. She had to wait outside in the sunshine for a little while and when we eventually spoke, she looked more rested and peaceful. We had the sun room to ourselves and the noisy world outside doesn't penetrate it. She said "You know I feel so much better now that I know that Jesus Christ was buried at Tyburn".

A loving mother arrived with her third child, the elder two having been periodic attendants. She was as immaculately dressed as her sisters. Endeavouring to offer stability to the youngest, I tentatively mentioned that regular attendance could bring financial assistance, but if she persisted with the previous expensive pattern, the hourly payment was to increase to £2.50 per hour. "Darling", she replied, "the kids only leave me when I'm working and I'd be exhausted if they came daily. Don't worry about the charges, I've just gone up myself from £40.00 to £70.00 per hour."

The children came from all sorts of backgrounds: British, European, African, Arab, Asian, as well as American; from the business, theatrical and diplomatic fields. We had one Russian child, long before the cold war ended and the Wall came down. A most unusual event in those days when they were all coralled in Highgate. We had Arab and Jewish children at the height of their confrontation, with never a cross word between them. We had the children whose parents had been given free or aided places. But our confidentiality was so good that we attained the objective of no one ever knowing which the financially aided children were. The tranquil and total commitment of the staff and the complete relaxed happiness of the children as they played in the lovely garden or did their special tasks in the sunny classrooms are an enduring joy to behold.

When the Church Commissioners eventually finalised the ninety-nine year lease of the Long Garden, it was in the name of the Hyde Park Nursery School Charitable Trust. The lease stipulated single occupation and was only for children or use relating thereto, but a waiver was permitted to allow the School and the Charity to share occupation, as the charity was indisputably "related", and we were permitted an access from our house in Archery Close into the Long Garden. These apparently minor complications caused grief and heart-ache when after my accident I had to pass on the management of the School with a view to the Charitable Fund selling it. The concept was simple, the Trustees would sell the shares in the limited company of the School while retaining the title to the land, and the legal position would be unchanged. However, our lawyers decided off their own bat to consult the Charity Commissioners who ruled that the School was itself a derivative charity and as such could not be sold. This was incomprehensible because the School had been a limited company years before the Charity existed, filing its accounts for tax and at Companies House, and technically it had always seemed to our advisers that the Charity held the shares as an investment. However we could not get the ruling changed and the Commissioners insisted the only route was a sale of the land and assets, which they decreed had to be externally valued at further great expense. Our lawyers drew a very complex and costly agreement with the buyer, maintaining the close link between Charity and the School, which allowed us and the Charity to continue access from our Archery Close house and to continue operations in the adjoining office, since these operations remained clearly related to the children in the School, as stipulated in the lease, and indeed wholly essential to some of them. Furthermore I also required access as I continue to be a consultant to the school. At each step of the legal negotiations our advisers told me they kept Chestertons fully informed and no problem appeared to be indicated.

Alas, by the time of completion the management of Chestertons had changed and with it their attitude. In spite of our telling arguments and the full support of Mrs. Pauley, the principal of Ravenstone House, the purchasers, they advised the Church Commissioners to stand on the legal technicality and exercise no discretion in our favour. Mr. Shaw of the Church Commissioners accepted the advice of his agents. It was a tragic result, but you can't fight a great corporation.

# CHAPTER SIX

It was very exciting to have the largest private garden in Westminster and I turned to the Manpower Services Commission (MSC) to help me with the task of maintaining it.

From 1978-83 the School had been working with the Youth Opportunity Programme for 16-18 year olds, YOP's for short. It was part of the MSC's Special Programme Division, and run by Mr. M.K. Blythe in the London Area Office at Tavistock Square with David Baxter as the Staff Officer Training, and Tim Mart and then Tony Dickens as Link Officer. Mrs. B. Webb was the Grants Officer and Katherine Quigley Internal Training Officer.

All these chiefs and not an indian, unless that was the name they gave the students. The students came to us from the Paddington Careers Office or St. Marylebone Employment Office, having been at the local comprehensive schools of Quinton Kynaston and St. George's.

In five years we had twenty five young girl trainees and all but one achieved their goal of entry to a Nursery Training College. The odd one opted for a career in hairdressing. So the system did work. For three years Kay Munro signed their attendance cards and placed them with a member of staff. Sue Richards was one such trainee and after obtaining her N.N.E.B. returned to the Hyde Park School to work with the younger age group with whom she is patient and kind. She and Kay Evans, Miranda Trafford-Roberts and Deborah Rodney of the Hyde Park School staff are still with Ravenstone House. Their classrooms still are cleaned by Mrs. Ellen Brade the tidy and reliable worker from Montserrat.

In any one week time was spent by the YOP trainees on sewing, laundry work, cooking, cleaning, child care and "Life & Social" skill classes. This latter meant learning to take messages, answer the phone, practise mock job interviews, and learn nutrition, simple tax and national insurance as it applied to them. One day a week a visit was organised to a bank, post office or tax office.

For the last two years Margaret Greaves competently ran the scheme, but other staff at one of those memorable staff meetings felt that the extra work entailed did not justify us continuing. The new government legislation had radically altered the conditions and many more schools were entering the YOP training scheme, so youngsters had now got alternative opportunities.

The grant we received had risen over the five years from £110,000 to £129,300 per annum. I was quite sad at the decision because, having attended their week long staff and financial seminar, for which I was paid, I thought I might soon be called a chief too!

We had many school leavers wanting to help, but unless they could offer three terms, a condition I made for pupils too, I felt their presence could be disruptive to the peace I sought and we would become like the constantly changing world outside the gates.

Christina Niven, daughter of film star David, of "Guns of Navarone" fame whom we had visited in the south of France, came between her recording sessions, and when Casper Shand-Kydd was with us, his mother made tentative enquiries about Lady Diana Spencer, as a trainee teacher, but she wanted only a term before her engagement to Prince Charles.

Gillian Richardson was one such school leaver who worked at the School between 1979-81. Dr. Ian Richardson and his wife Joan had three sons and three daughters and live near us in Scotland. So Birdie, as she was called, knew all about child care. She returned three years later, joined our Manpower Services Scheme in stone masonry and married the supervisor Mark Paxton.

During our thirty years of caring for children accidents rarely occurred. Looking at the books, one in each classroom, left to record any accidents, a tumble in the playground or a fall from the climbing frame had regular mention. Charlotte Lurot collided with a swing and needed two stitches above her eye, James Profumo had nasty bruises and cuts. Being an adventurous young man he pulled over an iron gate which was lying horizontally outside the lower classroom and should not have been there. Our most serious incident happened in the first year, when the son of an ambassador was tragically murdered. Very late one evening the police rang the door bell and showed me a note from a member of staff to say he had cut his lip playing. They insisted that I, dressed in dressing gown and slippers, visit the Church hall and read accurately the record. The book was taken away, fortunately I must have sounded truthful and I heard nothing more about it for six months. They courteously returned the accident book and told us the chauffeur had gone to prison. He had been paid to be the assassin and chose this minor incident to precipitate his evil instruction.

The new partnership with Manpower Services, was much more ambitious than the Youth Opportunity Training Scheme. Up until now I had felt the school kept in employment half of the Westminster City staff in both the Planning and Social Services departments and three quarters of Chestertons. In the Manpower Services Commission, I discovered a hierarchy which ensured every penny of my taxes were fully used. Piers T.T. Johnson was the Principal Project Officer of North London Community Task Force, a division of the Community Programme Centre which was found on the seventh floor of Lothian House, Market Square, Preston.

The principal staff officer, Mr. A.C. Coates visited the school in May 1985 with staff officer Mr. S. Hutchins from Unit 401, 8a Whites Row, Spitalfields, London. He had come twice previously to see us firstly in May with Mr. Tony Smith and then with Mr. Alan Barr on the 9th June 1983. At that time six short term unemployed young people came with a supervisor and helped to move and wash and repair the gravestones and remove no fewer that seventy skips of rubbish from the body snatchers' walk. Robert Bezzia who for the last twenty-six years, with his team from the Westminster City Council's refuse collection department supervised the departure of each load. Here I have a tale to tell of the walkway which surrounded the burial ground, erected by the Parish Council of St. George's Church, outwith their graveyard in the mid 19th century. The burial ground was then already nearly full but the demands by hospitals, for corpses for disection, was so great, as the Rev. W.A. Atkins writes elsewhere, that a watch house had to be built. Following the second world war bombing, the path had been closed at each end, for safety reasons. Inspectors of every kind were thick on the ground, including Mr. D.R. Campbell from Westminster City Council. Permits for the care of children do not come without numerous certificates and these were not obtainable with rubbish, in places, ten to fifteen feet high, inside the walkway. As long ago as 1968 I started to send copies of this request to my Connaught Street neighbours, Messrs. S. Turner, T. Parish, E. Hilleary of Wheelers, Mr. P. Chevalier of Pascal Hair and Beauty, Mr. Leach and then Mr. J.C. Beaufoy of New Holland Publishers, Mrs. Constantinidi of Face Place, Miss Sophie Beaumont and Mrs. Weinding flat dwellers, Mr. P. Miller the florist, Mr. Atwell the No. 31 Connaught Street statutory tenant, Mr. P. Dixon La Roche hairdresser, Mr. Rothman tailor, Mr. Hosseini of Creme Patisserie, Miss Whiteside of Jane Whiteside Dress Design, Mr. Michael Lawson the Vet, Renown Travel, Rare Book Ltd., Tropical Fruits, Daisy's Dress Shop. I wrote to each personally, asking for their financial or physical help to eliminate this pollution. No help or funds were forthcoming, so we started the task ourselves and, with the help of MSC short term unemployment project, in 1983 completed it.

I then claimed the freehold and many dusty books at the Church Commissioners were opened. In these lovely far-off days when the City of London and Chestertons stood by their word, an agreement was reached.

It was agreed if I gave up the freehold rights to the body snatchers' walk, they would grant a ninety-nine year lease of the land, which came to be known as the Long Garden. I did and they did, and shortly after the school received a supplemental lease in 1974 from the Church Commissioners for England for four feet eleven and a half inches of land, with instructions that no laundry may be hung there. The ninety-nine year lease incorporating all the free way was eventually signed in 1987 and back dated to 1983.

But I digress, Mr. Coates visited us with Tony Smith for quite a different reason two years later in 1985. With the power of bureaucracy behind them, I had been hoping his request for a licence for a building solely for twelve months for his team would be fulfilled. His wish was granted in May 1986 and so was ours. Hut No. 5 which had been used for storage was permitted to be enlarged. Further letters to La Patisserie, and access to the main electric cable, which ran through their basement, was granted. Pascal hairdressing gave access to the sewage, and Renown Travel to the water supply. We bought the hut, MSC rented it from us and on their departure, my proposal to apply for a new classroom in its place was accepted. Victory was ours!

The following MSC conditions were to be carried out by the long term unemployed whom Mr. Coates had put on the project.

"To repair completely the 500ft x 8ft wall bordering the long gardens of Albion Street on two sides. To mount forty grave stones on the garden side of the wall, to create a permanent monument to the Tyburn Burial Ground on which the Long Garden now stands.

The work will involve six skills:
1   Repointing the whole wall.
2   Demolishing one 14ft section and rebuilding it from the ground up.
3   Repairing several holes by bedding in new bricks.
4   Removing, cleaning and relaying about 50% of the saddle back coping bricks using new bricks where necessary.
5   Cleaning forty gravestones and affixing them to the wall.
6   Laying crazy-paving, made from poor quality gravestones, over an area at the Eastern end of the garden approx 40ft x 40ft in size."

The job description was to train one full-time and ten part-time Community Programme workers in stone masonry, brickwork and allied trades. The works managers specification proved more difficult to fulfil; reliability, honesty, punctuality and good attendance with an ability to write reports. They certainly needed the latter, and eventually fulfilled the former. Official paper streamed through the letter box like water off a mountain. Protective boots, gloves and clothing had to be bought. Offices were moved, guidelines changed and courses altered.

Unable to keep pace with the ever changing faces of unreliable supervisors, I felt compelled finally to qualify myself. In August 1982 I gained a City and Guilds London Institute Supervisors Award, with "experienced, committed and excellent" typed on the bottom. All that sweat and tears was not in vain.

The garden became cleaner and safer. Hut 5 glowed with activity. I mentally designed its replacement. The supervisors I remember were Paul Badger April '82, Hugh Wedderburn August '82, Mark Paxton, Alice Fletcher a skilled mason from Westminster Abbey and Tony Gallagher from my C & G Supervisors course November '82. Finally Stan Gothard a skilled and retired bricklayer brought our scheme to completion and helped fill in the forms, always in quadruplicate, for the new classroom.

It was Alice Fletcher who told me something I did not know about the Great Fire of London in 1666 which burned down St. Paul's Cathedral. When it was rebuilt, much of the money came not entirely voluntarily from Westminster Abbey, which is the Abbey Church of St. Peter, and thus started the common saying about "robbing Peter to pay Paul".

The scheme was upgraded, at a cost to the M.S.C. of £42,473.04. The trainees had classes at the Building Craft Training School in Great Tichfield Street, London. Fire Officers talked on every aspect of insurance cover. Mr. A.J. Francis from the Central Middlesex Family History Society spoke as did Mr. K. Mehers from the Environmental Health Office. Of the trainees, Mark Hebblethwaite from Coventry was most outstanding and was granted a place by Mr. J.H.W. Smith, at the Vauxhall School of Building and Further Education along with David Yerby. Fergus Colville trained on a short scheme in 1982, whilst his mother, Lady Colville of Culross was helping at the school, along with Glen Morgan,

Larry Tranquillan, Brian Cuffy, Patrick Smith, Nicholas Hills and John Manikuza, to name but a few of those who trained at the Long Garden.

One had to be dismissed for stealing money from staff coats. He was small physically and had to assert himself in other ways. With a personal penchant for red-heads, I nearly sent all my own children back for re-dipping, it gave me a special pleasure to have him. One day, four or five months after his departure, I was at the front door of the house in Somers Crescent and fumbling in my hand-bag for the keys when I became aware he was beside me. I put out my hand to say welcome when he grabbed me and took my hand-bag. My Scottish blood boiled as he took off down Somers Crescent and into Radnor Place and back up Hyde Park Crescent. I stormed after him shouting at the top of my voice "Stop Thief, Stop that Redhead, Stop Bag-snatcher". A car drew up beside me and the driver offered me a lift. I had almost caught up with him when he used a pedestrian short cut between Hyde Park Crescent and Connaught Street. I got out of the car and never saw the driver again to thank him. I could not even tell you the make of his car, his colour or name. I took off storming down Connaught Street still shouting. The publican of the Duke of Kendal stepped out at that moment and saw the young man hiding behind some rubbish bins and grabbed hold of him. My voice had been heard by the Vicar, as I passed St. John's Church. He was in running shorts and shoes and came up behind me and then raced ahead. The Vicar, the Publican and myself marched this boy to an area where we felt we could all sit together out of the cold. It was the front hall of the Southacre flats on the corner of Hyde Park Crescent. We called the police, and out of his anorak was produced my hand-bag. He had had no time to look inside it. The police knew him. He had been in their Juvenile Courts. He admitted "I have been there sixteen times before for bag-snatching". He was absolutely terrified this time, he thought he was in for slaughter. He knew the lingo, he admitted the theft and agreed he was not provoked. The police and he knew until his seventeenth birthday, he could not be sent to jail for the offence.

*1 Angus and Ishbel Macpherson; 2 A busy classroom at Somers Crescent; 3 Ester Smith and Margaret Hemsley; 4 Ester Smith; 5 A Christmas party; 6 John Arthur the chauffeur; 7 Joan Marsh with Angus and Ishbel; 8 Rupert and Georgina Mitford.*

*9 Andrew Impey and Alison Moss; 10 Marjorie Stevenson with Sheila Mallinson; 11 Kate Mitford, Adrian Spooner, Tarquin Gorst and Sheila Mallinson; 12 Guy Hollamby, Andrew Howland and Michael Mallinson; 13 Julian Grosvenor.*

*14 Ishbel and friends; 15 The gravestones in place; 16 Duncan; 17 The author and Duncan; 18 A class at St. John's Church; 19 Edward Saatchi; 20 The Nursery; 21 The School completed.*

*22 Sir Thomas Macpherson; 23 Joyce and Duffie Cowie and Tom Macpherson; 24 Facing south; 25 Balavil from the air; 26 Our Highland cows; 27 Robbie Gair; 28 The author; 29 Balavil; 30 Our dogs.*

*31 Sir Thomas Macpherson with the author, Angus, Ishbel and Duncan; 32 Lady Redesdale with Emma, Tessa, Kate, Victoria-Louise and Henrietta Mitford; 33 Angus with new puppy; 34 Duncan; 35 Ishbel; 36 Ishbel.*

*37 The Nativity at St. John's Church; 38 Sir Thomas Macpherson, Field Marshal Viscount Montgomery of Alamein and Angus; 39 Duncan; 40 Charles Cholmondeley; 41 Ishbel; 42 Joanna Cholmondeley.*

*43 The staff, children and Scots Guards at Wellington Barracks; 44 The children arriving at Buckingham Palace; 45 Somers Crescent and the New Hall in Hyde Park Crescent; 46 St. John's Church; 47 The Monument of the Tyburn.*

*48 Sir Thomas Macpherson with the author, Angus, Ishbel and Duncan; 49 Ishbel; 50 Duncan; 51 Angus; 52 Duncan and Tom; 53 Angus, Valerie, Tom and Lachlan.*

**15**

**16**

**17**

**18**

**19**

**20**

PARK
SERY

SCENT

HYDE PARK SCHOOL
ENQUIRIES & EMERGENCY SERVICE
01·262 1190

37

38

39

41

42

*Monument which stands in Hyde Park beside the Serpentine*

A Supply of Water by conduit from this spot was granted to the Abbey of Westminster within the Manor of Hyde by King Edward the Confessor. The Manor was resumed by the Crown in 1536, but the springs as a head and original fountain of water, was preserved to the Abbey by the Charter of Queen Elizabeth in 1560.

On the conclusion of this scheme knowing I could apply for the use of Hut 5 for the School, now complete with water and electricity, I declined the alternatives offered for a new MSC scheme.

Having almost reached first name terms with all who entered the MSC building, I started to renew my acquaintance with the Westminster City Council. The first sortie was in June 1986 to the Director of Planning and Transport Mr. J.R.G. Thomas and in July to Mr. D. Mathews, the Assistant Planning Officer.

Drawings of water, sewage and electricity routes, were given to John Hollamby of Chestertons. The MSC trainees had erected a hut, varnished doors and window frames and learned to look after their tools, had plastered the internal walls, put in a lavatory, basin and storage tank, made a tool box, a bench and shelving. English and spelling were taught by writing out the names of the tools used that day. The scheme brought great benefits to the land and the neighbourhood. Rubbish had gone, peace was returning, the roses, honeysuckle and berberis were showing growth and colour and Paul Simpson came regularly to clean windows and help around the place.

In the summer the "Friends of Hyde Park School" held a very successful fete, but the noise upset Hugh Barker, the manager of the adjacent flats, who served an injunction against us for loud noise from the electronic music, which I think was justified. We had a good working relationship with our neighbours and they supported the application for our planning and school licences to be changed from temporary to permanent ones. These were granted in 1988 by the London Borough of Camden and W.C.C. Planning Department and the W.C.C. Social Services Department of Area 5, Leighton Road. What a relief. When Camden wrote acknowledging their permit they demanded the picture on the front of our prospectus, a black and white of children playing, be changed to include ethnic minorities and not show trains for boys and dolls for girls, and to eliminate a gollywog with which one child was playing!

So the final expansion went ahead. The MSC hut was added to the existing Gate House as a new classroom, and where it had stood was erected a splendid new classroom for older children, an office for the charity and a meeting room.

# CHAPTER SEVEN

A SUDDEN CHANGE

Following a car crash on the seventeenth of August 1987 it soon became evident that I would be unable to continue with my career. My husband, as Chairman of the Charity, decided it would be in the best interest of the School that I step down as Principal. We had grown together for twenty five years. That year my twin sister, Councillor Anne Mallinson, became Westminster's Lord Mayor and I offered the School to Westminster City Council. When they reviewed the School's finances they felt the £150,000 cost for the new buildings which were being erected after the purchase of the ninety-nine year lease from the Church Commissioners unacceptable, so a sale on behalf of the Hyde Park School Charitable Fund, for the benefit of the children it aimed to help, was considered the best solution.

I have no recollection of the accident or of being taken to the West Highland Hospital in Oban. I awoke to the sound of Highland voices discussing the sheep sales which had taken place that day. How marvellous I thought, that God should have chosen this most musical of voices. The voices floated in and out of my consciousness and the word "wet" seemed to be regularly mentioned. In answer to a question I replied "surely this is not the time to discuss the divisions in the Tory party – I have a sore head and ribs and will you please stop prodding me". Everyone laughed and my "wet" bed was changed.

The day before leaving the hospital I rose from my bed for the first time. My head was uncomfortable, but it was my feet on which I had to concentrate as I walked to a small sitting area nearby. Several men appeared and a young doctor pointed at me and said "This is the one I looked after, she has cracked her head and ribs". Knowing all about my head injuries, I asked him to tell me just how many ribs were damaged. On hearing this the driver, who was in shock in the next bed, started yelling and screaming, "She's only bruised

103

and is in here to keep me company". I never did learn the number of damaged ribs I had as I changed the topic to one of going home. "A busy household and excellent help can look after me", I said and "both my husband and son are soon to leave for foreign parts". Within two days of returning home on the twenty seventh of August, the family left. My husband had asked the Kingussie doctor to call, as he was concerned at the size of the indentation in my forehead.

Trying to return to normal life, I was tackling the school accounts which were typed and ready to be sent out, as soon as I had enclosed a card of welcome to each new child. It was hot and sunny and I was sitting on the terrace. I found direct sunlight gave me eye strain, and without the sun I could not see what I had written. Dr. Mort found me sitting there, and he arranged a visit for me to an opthalmologist. He seemed disgruntled at being called out, bouncing up and down in front of me, listing the many other calls on his time.

On Monday the twenty first of September there was the Staff Meeting of Hyde Park School, and as usual I was in the chair. It soon became apparent that even having taken the precaution of travelling two days earlier from Balavil I was not able to carry on with the administration. The Headmistress, Administrative Secretary and the other eighteen members of the staff were kindness itself. I agreed a term's sabbatical was necessary for me but I was never to take up the reins again.

By appointment I floated into Dr. O'Hare's surgery in London. She had taken me from her predecessors, Doctors Ann Peach and Ann Thomson in Connaught Square. They both had Scottish connections and had been a great help since our own beloved Dr. Kennedy had a heart by-pass operation and had to retire. After twenty five years of running Hyde Park School, to discover I was mentally incapable of collating thought was a great shock. During my consultation with Dr. O'Hare I began to have the same sensation as I experienced with Dr. Mort, I was wasting valuable time. However my cry for help was heeded and an appointment with Dr. Lees was made.

It was one week after leaving our home of twenty nine years in Somers Crescent for a small mews house in Archery Close at the bottom of the School garden that the Spring Term Staff Meeting of 1988 was held. The new school buildings were about to be put into use, increasing the numbers from seventy five to one hundred. It was a very important meeting, but my words of guidance were inaccurate, poorly planned and above all, I was in continuous pain. The day before, my second and third vertebrae locked. After an unforgettable period of intense agony, Dr. Wynn Parry at the Royal Orthopaedic Hospital brought relief. He was an ex-RAF specialist considered outstanding in orthopaedic medicine, and he had also been my husband's predecessor as Prime Warden of the Worshipful Company of Dyers in the City.

A holiday away from it all was finally recommended. I heard my great friend from the Isle of Arran was off to lose weight. Shrublands Health Clinic found me a place with her for ten days. I myself lost one stone and still came back half a stone heavier than I had ever been in my life. I could not believe I could have become so obese and yet so uncomfortable was my body I did not realise my clothes may have been adding to the problem.

The following month I went to Texas and Florida for sun and sea, staying with our good friends Sara and Bill Bryce in Georgetown, who were kindness itself, and with Sir Ian and Lady MacGregor in Palm Beach where Dr. Benold manipulated my neck after another stiff and painful night. I was still wearing a collar and my enthusiasm for everything was negative. The MacGregors were infinitely patient. We had been friends since Ian became chairman of the Coal Board and appointed Tommy as one of his non-executive directors to see through the huge changes and improvements he was determined to institute, even while the famous strike was being defeated. Ian has just celebrated his 80th birthday and is as full of energy and wit as ever.

Autumn 1988 found me still lurching from one crisis to another. The increased workload caused by the increased number of children was a situation with which I was personally unable to deal competently. Christmas at Balavil, our first grand-child's christening, my two sons' birthdays and Hogmanay parties passed in a blur. I visited Kingussie's Dr. Mort in December and early January, at which time he handed out antibiotics. I returned to London on Twelfth Night, having had eighteen beds full every night.

By the twelfth of January my lungs were defeated and I rang Dr. O'Hare who recommended an X-Ray. Pleurisy and fluid were present. Kay Munro attempted to limit my activities, which on the whole were useless anyway. With my troublesome arm, back and neck I began to feel this long period of self centredness was becoming a habit. Miss Jan Spencer's physiotherapy at the Sportsman's Clinic, 71 Park Street was comforting and finally successful.

Having always had the self-confidence, self-reliance and ambition that comes from a good education, a sound Christian up-bringing and enjoyment from improving the lot of others, I felt until now that I had a happy, fulfilled life, with time for music, work and pleasure. Leisure is a word my husband does not understand as he puts as much energy into sport as he does into work or entertainment, and I tended to follow his example. Riding, reading, playing the piano, walking or home management bringing equal pleasure.

The accident has been enormously time consuming with doctors' reports and treatments, and with lawyers and paperwork greatly encroaching into my private life. My day starts off with a hot bath, which I have been known to approach on all fours when I am very stiff. I used to have my bath after nursery tea, and then change for dinner. Now dinner arrives before I have completed my day!!

For the first time since my marriage, I kept no accounts for the farm, school or trust for six months. This inevitably caused a loss of fees and extra costs and over reaching of budgets. During this time the school was like a ship without a master.

I failed to take full command of the move from Number 4 Somers Crescent to Number 27 Archery Close. Almost thirty years of possessions accumulated in ten bedrooms eventually required a removal van every Monday for two months!! Two of the loads went to Balavil, which is not just round the corner. Fate was not kind on this move. We took possession of 27 Archery Close just before Christmas, newly decorated and carpeted, and came back after New Year to find every floor under water from a burst tank in the roof, so we had to start all over again! The only nice thing was the discovery in the basement wall of a mile post which we have restored to legibility, reading "London 1 Mile" – the distance to Hyde Park Corner.

In my capacity as Foreman for the Hyde Park School's new buildings, the poor detailing of planning permits caused the new building to be built over a Tyburn tributary. The Tyburn water suddenly started to spout thirty to forty feet into the air much to the consternation of the people around. It had never occurred before, and was due to the construction team pouring cement in for the foundations of the new building. What happened was the pressure had split the medieval wooden hollowed tree-trunk. One of the conduits of the Tyburn joins up to the Serpentine in Hyde Park. There is a monument there stating that an Act of Parliament in 1349 gave the Abbey of Westminster fresh water supplied by the Tyburn Spring in perpetuity.

So we had to bring back the contractors to uplift all the concrete that had been put in. We then had to dig down sixteen feet below the foundations where we found the old wooden pipe and replaced it with new ones. Very carefully the coffins were moved sideways so that they remained at proper depth and needed no reburial. A design of a concrete floating raft foundation was insisted upon by City Hall, strong enough to carry a five storey block of flats, my surveyor said. Even to this day I still have a memento of that incident as I was able to retain a piece of the wood from the old wooden pipe and had it made into an ash tray which over the years has hardened and densified.

In the new buildings I then wired up the plugs for the radiators, a job I used to do almost every day, on the strength of my Certificate from the Electrical Association for Women. Both radiators caused fires big enough to call out the Fire Brigade!

At this time my capacity for social life was nil. We were moving and I packed up some of my favourite possessions in an anonymous plastic bag and took it to Scotland for safe keeping, and it still has not been found.

Before the accident my regular monthly journey of five hundred and twenty five miles between my homes, I undertook easily by car, only taking half a day. I would either set off at 6 or 7 a.m. and arrive in time for a late lunch, or had an early lunch and arrived for dinner. In the car came the children, dogs, food, flowers, as well as clothing from one house to the other. Now travel is by public transport, expen- sive and slow. To fly I leave the dogs, or if I go by British Rail arrival time is uncertain and buses cannot do it in a day. Having no disease which will kill me, and a family history of centenarians, I have a long future ahead. I had envisaged an interesting old age as an Elder of the Scottish Kirk, a Guardian at The Royal Caledonian Schools and an Administrative Member of the Y.W.C.A. A wide number of opportunities in many fields, and a highland life where fresh air and exercise do not have to be artificially sought.

The School, with a continuous flow of children, beautiful grounds, and staff free of problems, I had fitted in as my morning activity. In London, theatres, shops and friends filled in my waking hours. A loyal and kind husband, who, like the children, seemed to respond to the herd instinct. Either they were present, plus six for dinner or not there at all. Spare time I used to fill in library book forms, intervention butter returns, V.A.T., P.A.Y.E., or timetables. Christmas cards and presents for my eight brothers and sisters-in-law and their children is quite time consuming too. Just sitting here and listing them makes me feel weary.

This obsession with myself made me boring to friends, and without energy for social life, the art lost of making people sparkle.

The School, no doubt, would have had to go at some time, but I know several people of eighty making useful contributions to education. I wrote a farewell letter to all the Parents and now reproduce it here:

"Dear Parents,
Nearly thirty years after I founded Hyde Park School I am now handing over its ownership and management to Ravenstone House. I have seen with admiration the standards they keep and I have no doubts that at Hyde Park School they will keep up the high standards and high ideals which we have always had. I am delighted that I shall not be losing touch completely with the school as they have invited me to continue as a Consultant.

You will be aware that ownership of the School was in 1977 handed over to a charity for children, the Hyde Park Nursery School Charitable Fund. The Charitable Fund will continue at 27 Archery Close and will benefit from the transaction by a small regular income which the Trustees intend, as far as possible, to continue to use for children of this neighbourhood in less fortunate circumstances who attend the school.

The baby I started in 1962 and molly-coddled through its teenage years has now matured into a large and lively adult with many years of life ahead of it."

Hyde Park School ended abruptly, not only for myself but for all the people with whom I worked. They gave me the impression that I was totally immortal and I certainly thought I was. This way of life ceased on the seventeenth day of August 1987, when after having a picnic with their grandchildren at Ian and Sybil MacGregor's home on Loch Fyne in Argyll, I was being driven back to Balavil in a Volvo car, which I believe suddenly went up on to the bank at the side of the road to avoid a lorry and then was struck by several other cars – I remember nothing of it. Both the driver and myself were taken off with several from other cars involved to the hospital in Oban. This accident spelt the end of my career. Owing to a problem with balance, I did not hear what other people said as I was so busy adjusting from my dizziness that by the time I collected myself together I had paid little attention to what had been said to me. So the Headmistress took over the care of the children and the Administrative Secretary, Ann Saunders, with her quiet and confident abilities took over the management of the School.

The Hyde Park Nursery School Charitable Fund started the changeover to the Ravenstone House Group from Milton Keynes in 1988 first by management transfer and then by sale, and it was completed in February 1991. Now I am gradually picking up the threads of family life and other, I believe, useful activities, mostly in the service of young people and health care. With the loss of the school, garden and the home where we brought up the children it has been a hard adjustment, but defeat is not in my vocabulary.

Defeat is not in the vocabulary of Percy Reay either. He had been my father's closest friend in Edinburgh in 1914 when they both went off to the First World War with the Royal Scots. After the war they both moved to found new business enterprises in Manchester. When I was born Uncle Percy became my godfather, childless, a widower and an excellent tutor in all aspects of life. He is now over a hundred years old and remains my Uncle Percy with me as his honorary niece. His real nephew, my honorary cousin, is Willie Purves, now chairman of the Hong Kong Shanghai Bank. Willie and I were born in the same year, married in the same year, had children in the same year, and he and I have a real empathy. He is one of the most determined and courageous personalities I have ever met. He won a D.S.O. when with the Kings Own Scottish Borderers in Korea – the only National Serviceman ever to do so. His mother possesses them too, for despite having broken both her hips, at ninety she still lives alone in Findhorn Place, Edinburgh.

We have often been his guests in the fascinating oriental world of Hong Kong where my husband showed frequent skill in timing his business visits to coincide with the famous rugby seven-a-sides!

The Far East was a regular travel destination for us as my husband was for many years chairman of Louis T. Leonowens, based in Bangkok and covering all South-East Asia, and also of a company in Australia. Everyone has heard of that lovely sentimental musical, "The King and I". It was loosely based on real history, and the "I" was Anna Leonowens, whose son Louis was granted the trading concessions that developed into the firm my husband controlled. It enjoyed great historic prestige in Thailand – partly because Louis in his old age had immense stamina and a capacity much admired by the Thais for women, brandy and gambling.

When "The King and I" was running in London we invited the stars, Yul Brynner and Anna Neagle, to lunch with the Thai ambassador at Somers Crescent to hear something of the true story, and a delightful party it was.

By chance, my husband, after Leonowens was taken over by another company, became chairman of Boustead, also a famous Far East house, so we can still visit that delightful part of the world.

Such possibilities, together with my love of the Highlands and the support of friends like Percy Reay and Willie Purves have served to help me when I felt really down. But I promise you the abrupt change in my life has been hard to bear.

# CHAPTER EIGHT

THE NEW LIFE OF HYDE PARK SCHOOL

Tidying up time has come, the day is over. With fourteen large boxes I boarded the sleeper train to our home in Invernessshire. In them were the papers that created Hyde Park School. How right John Hollamby was when he declared in 1962 that much paper would flow before completion.

Over four hundred letters were written between our solicitors, Jaques & Lewis and Chestertons and I list some of the people I remember meeting in connection with the leases, licences and buildings at St. John's Church and the Long Garden.

*Chestertons*

Mr. John Hollamby
Mr. Steven Lee
Mr. I.D. Taylor
Mr. A. Forbes
Mr. Giles Ballantine
Mr. N.C.M. Renny
Mrs. Fiona Way

Mr. C. Brian Rusby
Mr. N.A.S. Newberry
Mr. J.E. Danger
Mr. C. Oliver
Mr. B. Richards
Mr. Laybourne
Mr. L. Heaven

*Jaques & Lewis*

Mr. G.A. Yablon
Mr. C. Heaps

Mr. B.A. Greenby
Mr. H. Lewis

*Connaught Street Residents*

Mr. and Mrs. Fred Salisbury and William of William Mansell Jewellers
Mr. Royston Isaacs of Hogg & Sons, Chemists
Joan Constantinidi of Face Place
Miss McMorran of Jade Fabrics Ltd.
Mr. P. Chevalier of Pascal, Hairdresser
Mr. Leach of New Holland Printing
Jane Whiteside of Jane Whiteside Coutourier
Mr. Sarwar of Markus Coffee Specialists
Mr. E. Hilleary of Wheelers
Mr. Rothman, the Tailor
Mr. Patrick Dixon, Hairdresser
Mullet & Booker Estate Agents
Mrs. Shirley Cooper of Daisy Couture
Jeeves Drycleaners

Somers & Kirby, Butcher
Mr. Miller of Prewett Miller, Florist
Andreanoff, Delicatessen
Mr. and Mrs. Michael O'Reilly and family of Wallers Newsagents
Tara, Mickie, Mandy and John Morgan
Mr. J.H. Kenyon, of Kenyon Funeral Directors
Mr. M. Harvey of F. Hughes, Solicitors
Picolo Bar
Mr. Husseini of La Creme Patisserie
Michael Hollamby of Connaught Galleries
Handman & Collis, Garage
Renown Travel Service
Ann Lewin
Le Chef
Tropical Fruits

Sadly, a large number of these have recently packed up and left under pressure of the recession and of massive Chesterton rent increases, and too many shops are now empty.

No less prolific at writing was the incumbent of St. John's. With the increasing use of the Church, now hired out for film productions, Bangladeshi keep fit clinic and other varied projects, the Secretary has found life very complicated and on hearing the Charitable Fund had been asked to write the history of the school, my final letter from St. John's Vicarage was short. "I forbid any correspondence between us to be printed".

From its derelict state, the Church has had an impressive re-birth. Not only has the expensive and troublesome roof been repaired, Bill Salisbury of Mansell's Jewellers in Connaught Street, has made the old clock on the west face work. New carpeting in the Church, new glass doors replace the inner Victorian ones, new stained glass windows, and repointing of the brickwork too. It is a great pleasure to see the Rev. Thaddeus Birchard walking in procession along the streets of the parish so publically proclaiming Christianity, wearing different colourful raiments to suit the Christian calendar and we are all delighted that his energetic work has been recognised by promotion to Canon. Young boys of many nationalities fill the Vicarage; some we got to know, for latterly they have taken our nursery childrens weekly prayer meeting, learning the stories of Jesus together.

We are all proud and happy to be associated in all its Christian activities and in farewell I reproduce the message that was written for the Church magazine in 1985.

"Not many people in our changing population now remember that St. John's Church was nearly closed for good, with a prospect of demolition some 23 years ago. The Vicar in those days, the Rev. Lewis, looked out on a parish still devastated by war damage and post-war neglect, and counted himself lucky if a tiny handful of people came on Sunday to Church. He enlisted the enthusiasm of two energetic ladies, Mrs. Tom Beale, wife of the Economic Minister of the U.S. Embassy, later Ambassador in Jamaica, who then lived in Hyde Park Crescent and Jean Macpherson. They in turn found an expert and influential ally in

Ivor Bulmer-Thomas, Chairman of the "Friends of Friendless Churches" whose role was to try to preserve what could sensibly survive in our ecclesiastical architectural heritage and to encourage its active social purpose. Together, after cutting through a forest of red tape, they had several talks with the then Bishop of London, and finally it was agreed that a new vicar would be appointed on Mr. Lewis's retirement, and St. John's given a new lease of life. The condition was that a significant activity had to be set up in the Church which could draw the attention of the growing, if somewhat transient, local population to St. John's Church. It was agreed that something involving children and parents would be ideal.

At that time Jean Macpherson, herself a trained teacher, had in her house a small kindergarten class for her two elder children and a few friends. She was prevailed upon to take the bold step of turning this into a nursery school and becoming the principal tenant of the Church Hall, thereby bringing the life, interest and activity that had been laid down as pre-conditions for the survival of St. John's Church.

All this went on under the vigorous eye of the Prebendary George Chappell of St. James's Church, Sussex Gardens, who had undertaken the supervision of the two parishes, until it was decided by the diocese that the best union would be between St. John's and St. Michael's, Star Street.

The rest is a history of success. An exceptionally energetic ex-Royal Navy captain, the Rev. Cuthbert Scott, was appointed vicar, installed personally by the next Bishop of London, Montague Stopford. After him came the Rev. Paul Rose, an outstanding musician. He was succeeded by the present incumbent, the Rev. Thaddeus Birchard. Under them St. John's had grown into the hive of parish activity it is today.

One of the main boosts to this programme was the building of the New Hall, still used by Hyde Park School, and it is an interesting illustration of the success of integrating Church and residents that the largest individual donor to the New Hall Building Fund, with a five figure sum, was an Arab parent of a pupil at Hyde Park School, who was happy to support a Christian Church because of its link with international child education. And the Hyde Park School is still proudly associated with the Hall where in September, 1985, it completed 23 years of partnership with the Church. Run by a charity, non-profit making, it has from early days taken in, free or aided, the children of less fortunate families, last year a total of 1,058 free or aided child days. Together, Church and School are beginning to form part of the history of the Hyde Park Estate."

About that time we had a problem over our noticeboard at the Long Garden. Bureaucracy showed its paces, following a written complaint to the local authority from the manager of the flats at St. George's Fields about its size. They had previously been sole users of the Albion Street access to the Long Garden and apparently wanted to establish their authority. The Council decided on the nameboard's removal without reference to us and I was obliged to appeal to the Secretary of State for the Environment. His report makes interesting reading. He wrote:-

"The sign is situated on a small triangle of landscaped garden adjoining the entrance to St. George's Fields from Albion Street which comprises two terraces of early nineteenth century four storey houses above basements faced in yellow stock brick with stucco dressings. Both terraces are included in the statutory list of buildings of special architectural or historic interest and the street forms an important part of the Hyde Park Estate.

St. George's Fields was originally the burial ground for St. George's Hanover Square. In 1968 part of the area was developed for a modern residential building in the form of a ziggurat surrounded by landscaped gardens. The Long Garden lies on the north side of St. George's Fields from which is separated by a chain link fence. The whole of the site lies within the Bayswater No. 5 Conservation Area.

*Grounds of Appeal:-*
The precise grounds for appeal are as follows:-
"The Emergency Service for Children under six years and over two years is unique in London. It offers a place (in an emergency) to any child in need, free, paying or aided by state or private charity. The notice is essential. To most it is the only notification of the site. Many have language problems or are so emotionally upset that a clear notice is the only guide they see. It has been up in its present position and site since the service opened in 1970 without it the service would be forced to close."

All the heavy guns were brought to bear and twenty two letters were written between April 1978 – 1980. Mr. Velivet and Mr. G.I. Lacy, the Chief Planning Officer of the Architecture and Planning Department, Westminster City Council, and Mr. P.H. Davies, Town and Country Controller of Advertisement Regulations agreed with Mr. C.I. Young on behalf of the Secretary of State for the Environment, Room

116

9/19 Tollgate House, Houlton Street, Bristol. Our sign was to remain, albeit a board a few centimetres smaller! This seemed to have settled once and for all our position in the Community.

Following the visit of Miss Daphne Bailey, Inspector of Westminster City Councils Social Service Department. the licence was granted by Mr. F.E. Fowler, M.I.S.W., F.R.S.H., for all the rooms in the Long Garden to care for seventy one children and thirty two in the New Hall in Hyde Park Crescent. The only requisite was Chest X-Rays for all staff every second year.

The Seymour Leisure Centre allotted our older children weekly instruction and use of the Council's Swimming Pool. The Friends of Hyde Park School had worked hard, happily and successfully to help to raise the money for the purchase of the land. The new building was complete, the school had one hundred pupils and from the many applicants to buy, the Trustees selected Ravenstone House, a Milton Keynes enterprise, run impressively well by the charming and efficient Mrs. Hilary Penley.

The time for farewell parties had come. The parents came with all the children festively dressed for a Pageant to represent the many years the land of the School had been in use. The Tyburn Axemen, Nuns, Prisoners of Newgate, Archers, Tennis Players, Gardeners and some plants too!! Finally the school band, ending with songs and a dancing display. My address at the Pageant on the tenth of July 1988 included the following:-

"Welcome friends. On behalf of the Trustees and myself thank you very much indeed for all your support over the many years the Hyde Park School has been in existence. You have all been marvellous neighbours, St. George's Church. St. John's Church, the shops and Colin and Ray of Linwood Builders whose craftsmanship created these buildings. Don Kemp, the tree surgeon whose artistry at cutting the correct branches has made the trees the landmark they are today. We have with us today three families who are the second generation to attend the school. The Mallinsons, Lurots and Munros. I would like to thank the Reverend Bob Callaghan, the Curate of St. John's Church for coming today and Mrs. Jean Burton, who was one of the creators and moving spirit of the Friends of Hyde Park School. The school owes a great debt of gratitude to the Church Commissioners and their Administrators, Chestertons, especially Mr. Hollamby, the late Mr. Danger, Mr. Heaven and Mr. Ballantine.

The Pageant today has as its Fear-an-Tigh, the Reverend Donald Wallace, resident Minister and a Director of the Royal Caledonian Schools. He is a Chaplain to Her Majesty the Queen. I have been a Guardian of his School for all the years I have had Hyde Park School. He and his wife and family have been a great inspiration and like the Head Master of Hill House, Colonel Stuart Townend, have guided me with sound and practical advice.

I do hope that you Parents will continue to enjoy the happy atmosphere of the School, now numbering a hundred pupils and that you will keep in touch with us through the Friends of Hyde Park School and continue to update us on the careers of your children. It has been a privilege to have had them in our care.

We say farewell to Mrs. Kay Munro who followed Joan Marsh in 1965. We owe her a great debt of gratitude and I am sure she has influenced all our lives. Joan Marsh moved to the Mitford family and is a pleasure to have with us today Dr. Emma Sody née Mitford and her son. Her mother, Lady Redesdale and Mrs. George Martin have for many years been Trustees of our Charitable Fund. The Trustees have been a great support to me and to the School.

Today there are sixteen full time and eight part time staff. The average length of service this day is five years and eight months for the full time staff, and when the part time staff are added the average is ten years and four months. This in a central City environment is a compliment to the way you have co-operated with each other, amongst these lovely gardens and created a good working relationship. I am proud to have been part of it.

The Pageant is about to begin, the eldest child is only five and a half. Please bear with us should any of the actors or actresses fail to remember their lines.

Thank you for coming, enjoy the occasion and have a happy lunch."

Four weeks later at a lunch in the new classroom with as many staff as could be present we gave Kay Munro a set of crystal hedgehogs to add to her collection. We wished her enjoyment of her well earned retirement and of her hobby of sailing. Also we confirmed that Ann Saunders had become Headmistress of this much larger school, under the management of the Milton Keynes company of Ravenstone House Ltd.

My taxi loaded with another pile of belongings for Balavil rushed for the train north, I was assisted by the most helpful driver to put it all on one trolley at Euston Station. As I turned to pay him, he had already started the engine. "You helped my son so much when we were going through difficult times, and he's now an accountant. I would not dream of being paid." I then recognised him as the father of an aided pupil at the school years before. Doesn't a happening like that make it all worthwhile?

# APPENDIX 1

YEARLY INDEX

**YEAR 1962**
ANGUS MACPHERSON
ISHBEL MACPHERSON
JULIET RONEY
MICHAEL MALLINSON
SIMON SESSLER
CHRISTOPHER EVANS
CAROLINE RAE
REBECCA BRODER
TOMAS TOMASCZYKI
WILLIAM RAMSEY
EMMA MITFORD
ADRIAN SPOONER
TEKLA SINGH
LAKY ZERVUDACHI
VIVIEN REYNOLDS
SABASTIAN CREWE
SABREENA CREWE
DAVID JACOBS
DAVID IRVINE
RODERICK BOWEN
JANE LANDAU
CHARLES WARNER
ANNE WARNER
JULIAN WILLIAMS
THERESA ANGELATOS
CLAIR LOGAN

**YEAR 1963**
WENDY VOS
LAKY ZERVUDACHI
CHRISTOPHER BOWEN
CHRISTOPHER GREGORY
KATHERINE BRESLER
THERESA ANGELATOS
CORINA HALL
LOUISE CUTLER
JULIET RONEY
ANGUS MACPHERSON
ISHBEL MACPHERSON
REBECCA BRODER
CAROLINE RAE
EMMA MITFORD
ADRIAN SPOONER
TEKLA SINGH
DAVID IRVINE
JANE LANDAU

CLAIR LOGAN
CHARLES WARNER
ANNE WARNER
JULIAN WILLIAMS
JULIAN GROVENOR
SIMON SESSLER
JAMES TRUMPER
DAVID SOPER
MARY FOSTER
CATHERINE COLE
SIMON HUGGINS
DOMINIC LUND
PUNCH HYDE-WHITE
JULIETTE HYDE-WHITE
IRIS LUND
JANE LIPERT
ANTHONY de la RUE
MARIA MASELLA
ANNA PALLANT
JONATHAN COOKE
LISA BROWN
MICHELE BERBAKOFF
ANDREW MACPHERSON
NICOLE ALLAN
CATHERINE RODRIGUES
CAROLINE RODRIGUES
SUSAN GALBERG
NICOLAS BRESLER
JANE CUTLER
RICHARD LEWIS
SARA BAIG
ADAM ROGERS
RICHARD COLLERO
TESSA MITFORD
JOCELYN TENNANT
AMANDA COOPER
SARA BAIG
NICHOLAS BRESLER
MICHAEL MIZRAHI
ROKI ITOH
JANE LANDAU
WILLIAM ROLLASON

**YEAR 1964**
ESMOND ROBINSON
MEG MOULTING
ISHBEL MACPHERSON

ANDREW MACPHERSON
JONATHAN CAPE
LOUISE SATURNIUS
JUSTIN STRATTON CHRISTENSEN
HELEN MALCOLM
NICOLE ALLAN
MICHAEL MIZRAHI
CAROLINE RODRIGUES
CATHERINE RODRIGUES
SUSAN GOLBERG
NICOLE BRESLER
KATHERINE BRESLER
JANE CUTNER
SARA BAIG
RICHARD COLLERO
JANE LIPERT
MARIA MASELLA
WENDY VOS
CHRISTOPHER BOWEN
CHRISTOPHER GREGORY
LOUISE CUTLER
TESSA MITFORD
JANE LANDAU
JULIAN WILLIAMS
SIMON SESSLER
JONATHAN COOKE
LISA BROWN
JOCELYN TENNANT
AMANDA COOPER
ANTHONY de la RUE
SIMON HUGGINS
ADAM ROGERS
RICHARD LEWIS
JOCELYN BROWN
SHEILA MALLINSON
SAGIT TEELUCK
STEPHEN DRANE
BENJAMIN FRIEDMAN
IAN ARMSTRONG
DAVID BEAN
ADRIAN ROGERS
JANE CUTLER
NICOLAS BRESLER
WILLIAM ROLLASON
SIMON SAVARESE
RICHARD GARDNER BROWN
DAVID CLARK
NICOLE PALLANT
GAVIN SASSON
KATE MITFORD
JOHN NEWTON
JEREMY KEARNS
STEPHEN LEWIS
SARAH AMBROSE
DANIELLA KOTTNAUER
AMANDA BALL
SANJIT TEELUCK

CLAYTON HODGE
MARCO SCARPATO
FRANCINO MACDONALD
LISA DALLAS
SIMON DAVIE
EDWARD DONNE
VICTORIA RICHARDS
KORRINA AGNEW
RICHARD AGNEW
HARRIET POSNER
SIMON SAVARESE

**YEAR 1965**
EDWARD DONNE
RICHARD GARDNER-BROWN
NICOLE TINERO
ALIX ROTH
ANNA MENMUIR
MARK PHILIPS
FRANCINO MACDONALD
DOMINIC LUTYENS
CORINA AGNEW
AMANDA HARRIS
CHARLES HARRIS
CLARE BARDSLEY
SARAH AMBROSE
ANDREW LORD HOWLAND
DAVID CLARK
NICOLE PALLANT
GAVIN SASOON
KATE MITFORD
VICTORIA LOUISE MITFORD
JEREMY KEARNS
ELEANOR MODY
SHEILA MALLINSON
SIMON DAVIE
CANDIA LUTYENS
STEPHEN LEWIS
VICTORIA RICHARDS
DANIEL KOTTNAUER
MARCO SCARPATO
RICHARD COLLERO
JONATHAN CAPE
ESMOND ROBINSON
HARRIET POSNER
STEPHEN DRANE
BENJAMIN FRIEDMAN
IAN ARMSTRONG
LOUISE SATURNIUS
CATHERINE HOPPER
ANDREW IMPEY
NICOLAS GALATIS
JOANNE GOLDRING
SARAH DARLINGTON
KOOKI ARBAB
JAMES GRIFFIN
RICHARD HOPTON

SEBASTIAN GORST
CHRISTOPHER YOUNG-TAYLOR
MARTIN YOUNG-TAYLOR
SIMON SESSLER
JOCELYN TENNANT
NICOLE ALLAN
WILLIAM ROLLASON
SIMON SAVERESE
JUSTIN STRATTON CHRISTENSEN
NICOLAS BRESLER
RIMA TE WIA TA
JACQUELINE MIDGEN
AMANDA BALL
GUY HOLLAMBY
ANN GERMING
DAVID Earl of MACDUFF
HELENA TEN BOS
MARCUS WILKINSON
ANNE BRICHTO
STEPHEN ARNOTT
RICHARD von ABENDORFF
SARA TRUMPER
EMMA DAVIE
RUDOLFO BARROS
ANGUS MACDONALD
  OF CLANRANALD
NICOLAS HECKSTALL SMITH
KARL STEINER
RUPERT TATE
JOHN MELAMED
GILLIAN LUSTY
SARAH BAIG
JULIAN HERVEY
HELEN MALCOLM
PATRICK SIEFF
SEBASTIAN RYKWERT
MARK GOATER
AARON FORBES
ANDREW HANSON
MATTHEW HARRIS


**YEAR 1966**
KATE MITFORD
VICTORIA LOUISE MITFORD
SARA TRUMPER
MICHAEL MITCHELL
RIMA TE WIA TA
MATTHEW HARRIS
MARTIN YOUNG-TAYLOR
CHRISTOPHER YOUNG-TAYLOR
MARCUS WILKINSON
MARK GOATER
STEPHEN DRANE
AARON FORBES
STEPHEN ARNOTT
PATRICK SIEFF
GILLIAN LUSTY

RICHARD von ABENDORFF
EDWARD von ABENDORFF
JULIAN HERVEY
RUPERT TATE
JOHN MELAMED
KARL STEIGER
POLLY JANE STAINSBY
BENJAMIN FRIEDMAN
JAMES GRIFFIN
NEIL INGLIS
NICHOLAS BRESLER
AMANDA BALL
VICTORIA RICHARDS
AMANDA HARRIS
CHARLES HARRIS
HELEN MALCOLM
RICHARD COLLERO
JEREMY KEARNS
JOANNA BOWEN
NICOLE PALLANT
ANNA MENMUIR
CANDIA LUTYENS
SIMON DAVIE
EMMA DAVIE
DOMINIC LUTYENS
CLARE BARDSLEY
JOHN JOACHIM
SARA BAIG
LUKE SIMKIN
TINA FEDESKI
ANN GERMING
ANDREW IMPEY
GUY HOLLAMBY
SARAH AMBROSE
ANGUS MACDONALD OF
  CLANRANALD
JONATHAN CAPE
SEBASTIAN GORST
DAVID Earl of MACDUFF
HELENA TEN BOS
JUSTIN STRATTON CHRISTENSEN
RUDOLFO BARROSS
NICOLE TINERO
EDWARD DONNE
SEBASTIAN RYKWERT
ANNE BRICHTO
ANDREW HANSON
SHEILA MALLINSON
PETER BULL
TARQUIN GORST
SVEN HELBLING
BETH POLLARD
VICTORIA ROBINSON
DAVID KENNEDY
EMMA KENRICK
ANDREW LORD HOWLAND
ROBIN RUSSELL

LORNE DARLING
TIMOTHY de LISLE
JOHN FEDESKI
LOUISA VIVIAN
NICHOLAS LAWSON
LUCINDA RALSTON
MARK PELHAM
LEE DECH
FIONA STEWART
LORAINE ROSSDALE
NATASHA HUGHES
NABILA KHASHOGGI
EDWIN RICHARDS
ARIANA ARNOTT
NORMAN LEVINKIND
MARK OHRSTROM
LIONEL WIGRAM
GEOFFREY BREITMEYER
GEORGINA HORLER
GILLIAN GOSLINGER
MONA OSMAN
CAROLINE MCTEAR
JANE MULLINS
JOANNA IMPEY
DONALD INGHAM
JOHN FEDESKI
JOHN PAUL YOUNG-TAYLOR
MARK ABBOTT
SERENA DONNE
MARK HANSON
JAMES GRIFFIN
JAN MIGUEL BARROS
PATRICK SIEFF
LOUISA VIVIAN
ROSALIND BEAVERS
JOANNA COHEN
ANNE BERRY
SALLY SPIERS

**YEAR 1967**
VICTORIA RICHARDS
EDWIN RICHARDS
MARK PELHAM
MARK OHRSTROM
FIONA STEWART
GEOFFREY BREITMEYER
LORAINNE ROSSDALE
GEORGINA HORLER
JACQUELINE HORLER
GIGI GOSLINGER
CAROLINE MCTEAR
LORNE DARLING
PAULA STEIN
TARQUIN GORST
DOMINIC LUTYENS
ANDREW IMPEY
DONALD INGHAM

CHRISTOPHER YOUNG-TAYLOR
JAN-PAUL YOUNG-TAYLOR
AARON FORBES
DANIELLE TINERO
CHARLES HARRIS
NICHOLAS LAWSON
MARK ABBOTT
EDWARD DONNE
SERENA DONNE
ANNE GOATER
RIMA TE WIA TA
NEIL INGLIS
MARK HANSON
JAMES GRIFFIN
JULIAN HERVEY
NABILA KHASHOGGI
ADAM PORTER
EVE STANDER
BENEDICT LOWSLEY-WILLIAMS
JOHN MELAMED
RODOLPHO BARROS
JAN-MIGUEL BARROS
EDWARD von ABENDORFF
RICHARD von ABENDORFF
AMANDA BALL
VICTORIA LOUISE MITFORD
MONA OSMAN
PATRICK SIEFF
MATTHEW HARRIS
MICHAEL MITCHELL
LOUISA VIVIAN
ANNE BRICHTO
ANGUS MACDONALD OF
   CLANRANALD
GILLIAN LUSTY
EMMA KENRICK
BETH POLLARD
SARA TRUMPER
LUCINDA RALSTON
EMMA DAVIE
ANNE BERRY
HILARY LLOYD PEARSON
IMOGEN COHEN
SALLY SPIERS
BASIL AKPABIO
NATASHA HUGHES
JESSICA TOTH
SOPHIE SWINEY
HENRY HAINAULT
SARAH SANDERSON
SERENA HOLLEY
SARAH SPIERS
LUCINDA SHAND-KYDD
FENELLA FOX
JAMES MULLINS
MARK MULLINS
JOLYON LUKE

MARCUS LUTYENS
POLLY ANNE BALL
NEIL INGLIS
EMMA GLASCOE
ANDREW LORD HOWLAND
ROBIN RUSSELL
JAN PAUL YOUNG-TAYLOR
FIONA STEWART
LORAINNE ROSSDALE
EMMA DONNE
MILES RAINES
HELEN BROWN
LYNETTE MARQUEZ
HENRY BROWN
JOANNA IMPEY
ANDREW BUDDEN
ALEX GOLDSMITH
ALICE STEWART-WILSON
HIROSHI KATAOKA
JOHN BROWN
JAMES CULLEN
VALERIE PIRES
GAVIN ROSSDALE
SIMON SIEFF
JESSICA FORBES
SERENA HOLLEY
CYBELE CLEVELAND
ANDREW MACDONALD OF
    CLANRANALD
SIMON GOODRICH
MARK HANSON
EDWIN RICHARDS
SARAD THAPA

**YEAR 1968**
IMOGEN COHEN
NICOLE de SONIER
URSULA McCARTNEY
ANDREW BUDDEN
DANIELLE TINERO
JUNE MATSUNOBE
JESSICA FORBES
TARA NEWLEY
THOMAS JUDSON
SARAD THAPA
FENELLA FOX
HELEN BROWN
POLLY ANN BALL
MARCUS LUTYENS
PAULA STEIN
SIMON GOODRICH
ANGUS MACDONALD OF
    CLANRANALD
LYNETTE MARQUEZ
DEBBIE BRADSTOCK
VICTORIA BENNETT
ANNABEL LORD

SARAH CURWEN
PENELOPE HARLEY
CAROLINE BEINDORF
SIMON SIEFF
JOLYON LUKE
JONATHAN FOREMAN
SASHA NEWLEY
SERENA HOLLY
SARAH HARVEY
LISA FRY
SARAH BARNETT
ANNE BERRY
MARK PELHAM
JAN PAUL YOUNG-TAYLOR
TARQUIN GORST
PATRICK SIEFF
EDWARD von ABENDORFF
SARA TRUMPER
MARKHAM HANSON
GILLIAN LUSTY
ROBIN RUSSELL
ALICE STEWART-WILSON
GIGI GOSLINGER
MONA OSMAN
LUCINDA SHAND-KYDD
JOANNA IMPEY
SARAH SANDERSON
VALERIE PIRES
EMMA LOUISE GLASCOE
MARK SERVAES
ANNA GOATER
NATASHA HUGHES
CYBELLE CLEVELAND
SERENA DONNE
ALEX GOLDSMITH
LUCINDA RALSTON
HENRY HAINAULT
SOPHIE SWINEY
HIROSHI KATAOKA
EDWIN RICHARDS
JAMES CULLEN
JOHN BROWN
AUSTEN KOPLEY
JONATHAN LEE
RICK KELLY
ALEXANDRA WATTS
LISA HUGHES
MARKHAM HANSON
BEATRICE DOT
SARAH-JANE BRYANT
NICOLE de SONIER
SOPHIE WIGRAM
TOM JUDSON
ALEXANDER ZAHLER
BETH POLLARD
EMMA GLASCOE
KATE GLASCOE

125

IAN CULLEN
ANDREW MACDONALD OF
  CLANRANALD
MELANIE GOLD
JAMES GORDON
LAURA LOUDON
DEBRA COOPER
MILES RAWES
BRIAN KEEFE
INGER KUHNE
BROOK HANSON
NICOLE BEINDORFF
JASON MASSOT
TIMOTHY QUINLAN
JASON LEWIS
LOUISE MOUDARRI
RIAD MOHAMED
HEIDI VAARDAL
ANNE BYNER
JAMES GORDON
MORGAN WATTS
ANNE GOATER
FIONA HARDY
ROBERT SASSON
MELANIE BERLIN
PHILIP BERLIN
MARY FABRICANT
JAMES HENDERSON
PAUL HARDY
ROBERT GORDON

**YEAR 1969**
LOUISE MOUDARI
JOLYON LUKE
PENELOPE HARLEY
JAMES GORDON
CAROLINE BEINDORFF
NICOLA BEINDORFF
JASON MASSOT
DANIELLE TINERO
ALEXANDER ZAHLER
BRIAN KEEFE
DEBBIE BRADSTOCK
URSULA McCARTNEY
SUSAN GAETZ
SERENA HOLLY
JONATHAN FREEDMAN
MARY FABRICANT
JUSTINE GONSHAW
PAULA STEIN
SUZETTE SWINEY
LAURA BIRNHAK
MARGARET BERRY
JONATHAN LEE
AUSTEN KOPLEY
CHRISTOPHER HORDERN
CHARLES BERGER

FENELLA FOX
NATASHA HUGHES
LISA HUGHES
SARAH HARVEY
JASON LEWIS
SOPHIE WIGRAM
IMOGEN COHEN
MELANIE BERLIN
PHILIP BERLIN
TOM JUDSON
HEIDI VAARDAL
MOHAMOUD ABDILLEH
ROBERT SASSON
MARCUS LUTYENS
KIM van DUYTS
QUELIN van DUYTS
HIROSHI KATAOKA
FODIL RAMOUL
BROOK HANSON
HITOMI ISHO
ANNE BYNER
LYNETTE MARQUEZ
RICK KELLY
INGER KUHNE
SIMON SIEFF
PAUL HARDY
DEBRA COOPER
HOPE BRADY
SARAH BARNETT
ANNABEL LORD
SARAD THAPA
KATE GLASCOE
SARAH BRYANT
RUPERT STRATTON
LAURA LOUDON
SIMON GOODRICH
EMAN ABU SAID
ROBERT GORDON
JONATHAN FOREMAN
MAXIMILLIAN WIGRAM
MARK BARETTO
ROLAND MALLINSON
SASHA NEWLEY
ISABEL VIEIRA
ANDREW ROTHEISSER
ALEXANDRA WATTS
MORGAN WATTS
ERIC LIBOCK
JONATHAN LITHIBY
TINA WHITMORE
DANIELLE TINERO
RUPERT LORD
FIONA HARDY
BETH POLLARD
DEBRA BRADSTOCK
ANDREW MACDONALD OF
  CLANRANALD

JONATHAN SIEFF
RICK KELLY
KEVIN GILRAIN
MARK GILRAIN
JUSTINE HOHNEN
BETTINA HOHNEN
ROBERT GORDON
ANDREW ROTHGIESSER
HEATHER KEEFE
NATALIE GOLDSTEIN
CAMILLA SIM
ALEXANDRA BADGER
ELIZABETH FORSSANDER
ALEXANDRA KONIALIDIS
SUSUMU KATAOKA
ALISON MOSS
HEIDI JOSEPH
KAY MONTGOMERY
ANDREW WEIR
ANNE-MARIE RANSOM
HELEN DOUNAEV
RUPERT LORD
JULIA COPE-THOMPSON
VICTORIA de LISLE
HENRY JODRELL


**YEAR 1970**
MARK BARETTO
CAROLINE BEINDORFF
NICOLA BEINDORFF
KEVIN GILRAIN
MARK GILRAIN
ANDREW MACDONALD OF
  CLANRANALD
URSULA McCARTNEY
SIMON SIEFF
JONATHAN SIEFF
RICK KELLY
LAURA LOUDON
RUPERT STRATTON
JONATHAN FREEDMAN
JASON LEWIS
JAMES GORDON
ROBERT GORDON
PHILIP BERLIN
SUSAN GAETZ
TINA WHITMORE
SUZETTE SWINEY
HOPE BRADY
MAXIMILLIAN WIGRAM
JULIETTE HOHNEN
BETTINA HOHNEN
ANNE BYNER
JUSTINE GONSHAW
JONATHAN LEE
ANDREW ROTHGIESSER
HEATHER KEEFE

LISA HUGHES
HEIDI VAARDAL
ROLAND MALLINSON
ISABELLE VIEIRA
INGER KUHNE
ALEXANDRA WATTS
MORGAN WATTS
ANNE DARER
ALEXANDRA BADGER
ELIZABETH FORSANDER
ALEXANDRA KONIALIDIS
HEIDI JOSEPH
CAMILLA SIM
CHARLES BERGER
LAURA BIRNHAK
NATALIE GOLDSTEIN
CHRISTOPHER HORDEN
SUSUMU KATAOKA
KAY MONTGOMERY
ALISON MOSS
ANNE-MARIE RANSOM
ANDREW WEIR
CARL-CHRISTIAN KITCHEN
AUSTEN KOPLEY
REBECCCA KOPLEY
CHARLOTTE MARTELL
JULIA COPE-THOMPSON
ANTHONY VRONDISSIS
RUPERT ENGLISH
EMMA ROSS
FRANCESCA PATEL
DAVID VORRINGER
MARCUS BLUETT
ROSALIE ENVERGA
CLAIRE HAMMOND
DAVID St GEORGE
HENRY JODRELL
LUCY WIGRAM
CAMILLA WIGRAM
RICHARD TARTARELLI
SASHA NEWLEY
ANNABEL SIM
RUPERT ENGLISH
CHARLOTTE MARTELL
MONA ISMAIL
YUSOF ZEFFRIALI
DEEPA NAIR
RUPERT MITFORD
LUCY POTTER
GILES DUNN
RUPERT LORD
JULIA GRIFFFIN
NANIA HERNANDEZ
ANNA DARVAS
GRANT BUTLER
CHARLOTTE CONRAD
CARA PRESSMAN

JONATHAN HYNES
CASPAR SHAND-KYDD
ALEXANDER McKENZIE
LISA JOSEPH
MICHAEL KLONARIS
ARIETTA LIVANOS
PHILIP DONALDSON
RODRIGO MARQUEZ
MARIO RODRIGUES
FIONA LOFTING
SACHA LLEWELLYN
HEATHER KELLY
SABINE MRUCK
CARLOS DOMINGUEZ
MARK LONGHURST
RICHARD TARTARELLI
EDWARD MUIR
IRENE CLEVELAND
LARA IVANOVIC
SAMANTHA THIRLBY
CHARLOTTE MARTELL
EMILY BLACK
SIMON BURNETT
ALLYSON ANDREWS
EMMA BOURNE
CLAIRINDA WEIR
PHILIP NARDI DIA
DANA MACMILLAN
DEBORAH STONE
JUDITH WALSH

**YEAR 1971**
MAXIMILLIAN WIGRAM
CAMILLA WIGRAM
LUCY WIGRAM
JONATHAN LEE
ALEXANDRA WATTS
MORGAN WATTS
ROLAND MALLINSON
ANNE BYNER
ANDREW ROTHGIESSER
JONATHAN SIEFF
JUSTINE GONSHAW
PENELOPE GONSHAW
ALEXANDRA BADGER
STEPHEN BADGER
NICOLA BEINDORFF
LISA HUGHES
DANA MACMILLAN
ALISON MOSS
INGER KUHNE
ANNE-MARIE RANSOM
ANDREW WEIR
GRANT BUTLER
CHARLES BERGER
JULIA GRIFFIN
SUSUMU KATAOKA

MARCUS BLUETT
SABINE MRUCK
AUSTEN KOPLEY
REBECCA KOPLEY
CHARLOTTE MARTELL
NANIA HERNANDEZ
ANNA DARVAS
YUSOF ZEFFRIALI
CARA PRESSMAN
LUCY POTTER
RUPERT MITFORD
EMMA BOURNE
RUPERT LORD
DAVID St GEORGE
CASPAR SHAND-KYDD
ALEXANDER McKENZIE
PHILIP DONALDSON
ANTHONY VRONDISSIS
RODRIGO MARQUEZ
JONATHAN HYNES
MARK LONGHURST
IRENE CLEVELAND
GILES DUNN
PIERS DUNN
LISA JOSEPH
MARIO RODRIGUES
MICHAEL KLONARIS
LISA SMITH
SACHA LLEWELLYN
HEATHER KELLY
CARLOS DOMINGUEZ
DEVANG JHAVERI
SEAN VAARDAL
SIMON BURNETT
JUDITH WALSH
ETIENNE BOURGEOIS
DEBORAH STONE
VICTORIA STRATTON
ALLYSON ANDREWS
AMANDA FOREMAN
ANTHONY DAWSON-ELLIS
JAMES HAMILTON
CARLOYN BUCSI
JULIA COPE-THOMPSON
CLARINDA GREIG
LARA IVANOVIC
ANNABEL EKER
ROBERT HARLEY
ELIZABETH MURDOCH
REBECCA BUNYAN
GEORGINA MITFORD
JUDITH WALSH
ANNABEL FROST
MARIO RODRIGUEZ
ANDREA MACMILLAN
AYALA de ZOBEL
CONSTANTINE TAYLOR

NICHOLAS JACKSON
CLARINDA WEIR
STEPHANIE ANDREWS
ANDREW HYNES
AMANDA SIMPSON
MARTIN BIRNHAK
STEPHEN RICHARDSON
ADRIAN DONOVAN
LAURA JANE ANTONIADES
PHILIP APOSTOLIADES
JONATHAN PYSER
BARBARA KOPLEY
ANDREW EDEN
ANDREW LAWSON
ARIETTA LIVANOS
WENDY KAY
EDWARD KESSLER
DARYL LEWIS
PATRICK BOURGEOIS
JONATHAN FAIMAN

**YEAR 1972**
STEPHANIE ANDREWS
LAURA JANE ANTONIADES
PHILIP APOSTOLIDES
ROBERT BECKMAN
STEPHEN BADGER
JAMES BETHELL
MARTIN BIRNHAK
PATRICK BOURGEOIS
EMMA BOURNE
REBECCA BUNYAN
SIMON BURNETT
CAROLYN BUCSI
MARK CITRON
JAMES DATNOW
PHILIP DONALDSON
ADRIAN DONOVAN
GILES DUNN
PIERS DUNN
ANNABEL EKER
ANDREW EDEN
JONATHAN FAIMAN
AMANDA FOREMAN
JOANNA FRASER
ANNABEL FROST
PHILIP FLACCOMIO
FERGUS GILROY
KATHLEEN GILMAN
TAMBORLAINE GORST
ROBERT HARLEY
ANDREW HYNES
JONATHAN HYNES
NICOLAS JACKSON
LIZA JOSEPH
WENDY KAY
HEATHER KELLY

JONATHAN KELLY
TEDDY KESSLER
REBECCA KOPLEY
BARBARA KOPLEY
ANDREW LAWSON
DARYL LEWIS
SACHA LLEWELLYN
MARK LONGHURST
CHARLOTTE MARTELL
SABINE MRUCK
JONATHAN PYSER
NADIA RAMOUL
STEPHEN RICHARDSON
CASPAR SHAND-KYDD
TARA SHEPARD
AMANDA SIMPSON
DEBORAH STONE
VICTORIA STRATTON
SEAN VAARDAL
ANTHONY VRONDISSIS
CLARINDA WEIR
LUCY WIGRAM
CAMILLA WIGRAM
NANIA HERNANDEZ
MAX HERNANDEZ
WILLIAM BETHELL
JANE BIDDLE
SIMON COPE-THOMPSON
CARLOS DOMINGUEZ
FATMA EL-SALEH
DIANE GOODMAN
KATHERINE KINROSS
CHARLES KINROSS
KARINA NG
KAREN O'DONOHUE
JAMES STRAUSS
HILARY WEHRLE
SALIM ADAMJEE
NICOLAS BEITNER
CHARLES BRYANT
REBECCA COPELAND
BABAK EMANI
JASON EKER
MATTHEW JOHNS
HANNAH GARRARD
DANIEL GOLD
CATHY IJSSELSTEIN
INGRID IJSSELSTEIN
EMILY JOHNSON
KALID JAVANI
DANIEL KELLY
ALEXANDER LEE
BENJAMIN LEON
JAMES LENGEMANN
ARIETTA LIVANOS
SCOTT LESTER
ANA-MARIA LOCKTON

NATHALIE PAPAGEORGHIOU
VIMI SHAH
ALISA TWISK
SIMON WOODMAN
AMANDA WOODMAN

**YEAR 1973**
LAURA JANE ANTONIADES
ALEXANDER BEEBER
NICOLAS BEITNER
ROBERT BECKMAN
WILLIAM BETHELL
JAMES BETHELL
JANE BIDDLE
PATRICK BOURGEOIS
CHARLES BRYANT
MARK CITRON
REBECCA COPELAND
SIMON COPE-THOMPSON
CARLOS DOMINGUEZ
JASON EKER
JONATHAN FAIMAN
PHILIP FLACCOMIO
AMANDA FOREMAN
HANNAH GARRARD
FERGUS GILROY
MICHELLE GEORITZ
DANIEL GOLD
DIANE GOODMAN
EMMA HYMAN
JAMES HYMAN
MAX HERNANDEZ
ANDREW HYNES
JONATHAN HYNES
CATHY IJSSELSTEIN
INGRID IJSSELSTEIN
MATTHEW JOHNS
KATE JOSEPH
EMILY JOHNSON
WENDY KAY
DANIEL KELLY
JONATHAN KELLY
TEDDY KESSLER
CHARLES KINROSS
KATHERINE KINROSS
DILLON KENNEDY
ANDREW LAWSON
ALEXANDER LEE
JAMES LENGEMANN
BENJAMIN LEON
SCOTT LESTER
DARYL LEWIS
ANA-MARIA LOCKTON
NATHALIE PAPAGEORHIOU
JONATHAN PYSER
MELISSA ROGERS
VIMI SHAH

TARA SHEPARD
JASON SIMPSON
JAMES STRAUSS
MELISSA THOMPSON
ALISA TWISK
SEAN VAARDAL
SIMONE WAKWELLA
HILARY WEHRLE
AMANDA WOODMAN
SIMON WOODMAN
SIMON WICKS
AMANDA SIMPSON
KHALID JILANI
DUNCAN MACPHERSON
PAUL SELLAR
CYNTHIA STELLAKIS
NICHOLAS BOURNE
VERONIQUE BOURGEOIS
PATRICK DONOVAN
MELANIE HITCHINS
PETER MANLEY
JAVIER MARTIN
TIMOTHY NISHIBORI
PETER RICHARDS
DANIELLE ROFFE
TOBY STRAUSS
NICHOLAS CORBY
HELMER ADAMS
HENRIETTA BALDOCK
ELINOR BALL
DAVID CANNON
GEORGINA FROST
SCOTT GARFIELD
KRISTAN KISH
NICOLAS KONIALIDIAS
BEVERLY LANGFORD
EUGENIE LIVANOS
RACHEL MARGOLIS
LISA MODET
RUPERT MORRISON
LAURA NISHIBORI
STEPHEN PACE
KRISTIN PAULYSON
MICHELELE PENA
PRYRA RANA
ANGELA REISSMANN
DANIELLE ROFFE
LEONORE SHARP
CHRISTOPHER St GEORGE
PETER TAFT
BENJAMIN WIGRAM

**YEAR 1974**
HELMER ADAMS
ALEXANDRA ALBION
HANAN ALLAF
RACHEL AQUILO

130

SAMANTHA ANGUS
ALEXANDRA ASHBOURNE
HENRIETTA BALDOCK
ELINOR BALL
NICHOLAS BEITNER
VERONIQUE BOURGEOIS
JASON BRIGGS
SUSAN CALVO
DAVID CANNON
MARISA COLLINGS
CYNTHIA DAVIS
KIRSTIN DEEVES
PATRICK DONOVAN
DAVID DUBOFF
JAZMIN DUBOURG
FOTINI EFTHIMIOU
ISABELLE FAVRE
GRESHA FEIFER
JAMES FELLOWES
LEE FREEMAN
GEORGINA FROST
TRACY GARFIELD
NICHOLAS GOLD
JAMES HANSCOMBE
JAMES HARRIS
AMYN HUDDA
GREGORY HUNTER
JAMES HYMAN
CHRISTOS IOANNOU
MARIA IOANNOU
SANDEEP JAIN
MATTHEW JOHNS
SIMON JOHNS
ANDREA JOHNSON
DAVID JONES
JOHNNE KARKI
MELISSA KENNEDY
MARK KESSLER
GARETH LANGDON
SHANA LANGDON
BEVERLY LANGFORD
JASMINE LASSEN
JULIAN LEE
POLINE LEMOS
SARAH LLOYD
GEORGE LOVERDOS
CHARLOTTE LUROT
CHARLES LYON
LANCE MALMGREN
VANESSA MASON
WALEED MONDANI
TIFFANY MOXHAM
JUSTIN NASH
LAURA NILSEN
KRISTIN PAULYSON
MICHELE PENA
LUCY PHILLIPS

JASON POWER
ANGELA REISSMANN
DANIELLE ROFFE
PAUL SELLAR
LEONORE SHARP
TRISTAN SIMMONDS
LAURA SOLOMONS
TOBY STRAUSS
SASKIA THORNTON
RACHEL TROOSTWYK
TOBY WALKER
SIMON WICKS
BENJAMIN WIGRAM
AMBEREEN YUSUF
DYLAN FARR
VICTORIA FROST
NICOLE GARCIA
JAMES KER-LINDSAY
GARETH LANGDON
LUKE LOCKHART
EUGENIE LIVANOS
GEORGE LOVERDOS
CHARLOTTE LUROT
MARK MICHAELS
KAREN McGRATH
ALEXANDRA PAPAGEORGHIOU
PRYRA RANA
ALEXANDER TERRY
KARYN von MATTHIESSEN
MAJED AL-MAJED
MOHAMMED AL-SABAH
JOANNA BARNETT
AANAL CHANDARIA
PARAS CHANDARIA
KATERINA EFTHIMIOU
AMBER FARR
MARIA FERNANDEZ
LOUISE FERNANDEZ
TAMARA GATWARD
DANIEL GORDON
JAGRATI JAIN
HEERA KAPOOR
CATRIONA MACDONALD OF
    CLANRANALD
JULIAN MARKS
MARK MICHAELS
FLORENCE MONSEAU
GREGORY PALMER
MURROUGH O'BRIEN
RANIA SHAMS
KELLY SINCLAIR
ALISON THOMSON
NICHOLAS WALTER


**YEAR 1976**
DOLORES ABBOTT
RACHEL AGUILO

JOANNA BARNETT
MATTHEW BRENER
PAUL BRIGGS
AANAL CHANDARIA
PARAS CHANDARIA
LUCY CONSTANTINI
GENO CHOUCAIR
YVETTE CROMPTON
GEMMA DEEVES
MARY ELLEN DONOVAN
ALEXANDER EDMONDS
KATERINA EFTHIMIOU
CHARLES FELLOWES
GRESHA FEIFER
TAMARA GATWOOD
NICHOLAS GOLD
SARAH JANE GOULD
TIMOTHY HART
FRANCES HARRIS
HADLEY HUNTER
JAGRATTI JAIN
SOPHIA JUNDI
MILICIA KENNEDY
JAMES KESRUANI
ALEXIA KLEONAKOS
PANDELIS LEMOS
LUKE LOCKHART
JULIAN MARKS
ALEXANDER MASSEY
LARA MASTERS
DUNCAN MCGRATH
JOANNA MEYER
AMANDA MILLER
MARK MICHAELS
SAMANTHA NIX
MURROUGH O'BRIEN
GREGORY PALMER
CHRISTINA PARDAL
SAMUEL PARKES
ADAM PERRY
JEROME PINSENT
CHARLOTTE POLIZZI di
  SORRENTINO
DAMIAN RAYNE
JOHN RIOS
NATASHA ROFFE
MANOLIS SAKELLARIOS
NATALIE SALVATORI
KATE SAUNDERS
LEONIE SCHRODER
RANIA SHAMS
FABIAN SHARP
KELLY SINCLAIR
DINA TAYARA
ALEX TELNIKOFF
VICTORIA TOMPKINS
LOUISE TROOSTWYK

KARYN von MATTHIESSEN
NICHOLAS WALTER
DOMINIC WHITING
DEBORAH WOLFSON
DANIEL WRAY
COLETTE ST CLAIR
DAMIAN ANGUS
BRETON BATTENFELD
SERGIO BEGGIATO
JOHN CLOSS
MICHAEL HANANIA
SAMUEL HART
FLETCHER HOROBIN
MARIO NUZZO
HARRY RAMBAUT
LEONIE SCHRODER
NABBY SOUFRAKI
WATTY SOUFRAKI
COLETTE ST CLAIR
ANDREW WILLIAMS
HANOUF AL-MAJED
OLIVER BEDACK
FLEUR BRENER
AMREETA BUXANI
JOHNNY FRANCISCI
DANIEL KESSLER
POPPY LILLEY
JEAN LORRAINE
CAMILLA MARCEL
AHMED MOHARAM
MICHAEL NOTT
SAMUEL PARKES
VISHAL PATRAO
JEROME PINSENT
ELINOR RIDDELL
GAYLE ROBERTSON
ANGELIQUE SWANEPOEL
LAURA WALSH
DANIEL YEFET
NABBY SOUFRAKI
WATTY SOUFRAKI
GUY LORRAINE
GENNA PRESTON

**YEAR 1978**
DAMIAN ANGUS
BRETON BATTENFELD
SERGIO BEGGIATTO
OLIVER BEDACK
FLEUR BRENER
MATTHEW BRENNER
AMREETA BUXANI
JOHN CLOSS
LUCY CONSTANTINI
YVETTE CROMPTON
MARY ELLEN DONOVAN

MICHAEL GEHA
RAMI GHANDOUR
TALAL GHANDOUR
DAVID GINSBERG
MIRANDA GLASSER
ROLAND GLASSER
CLAIRE GOLD
SAMUEL GORDON
JUNIOR HABIS
FLETCHER HOROBIN
DANIEL KESSLER
MARK KIKANO
PETER LAWN
LUKE LEANDER
SOPHIE HAWKEY-EDWARDS
MARIKA LEMOS
XENIA LEMOS
CHLOE LILLEY
POPPY LILLEY
KATE LOUSTAU LALANNE
OLIVER LUROT
CAMILLA MARCEL
POLLY McCOWAN
BRIAN McRAE
CHIARA MENNINI
AHMED MOHARAM
ANDREW MURDOCH
ALEXANDER NIX
MICHAEL NOTT
CHRISTINA PARDAL
SAMUEL PARKES
MARK PARKINSON
TAYMOUR POLDING
GENNA PRESTON
OLIVER PROVENZA
DAMIAN RAYNE
NATASHA ROFFE
MAXWELL SHILLINGLAW
DAVID SYKES
JULIAN SOPER
ROBERT SOPER
ANGELIQUE SWANEPOEL
MAYA TAYARA
ALEX TELNIKOFF
SEVERINE TEURLAI
GEORGE VLOTIDES
JAMES WALTERS
BRENDAN WALSH
LAURA WALSH
MUNA WEHRLE
BEN WOODIWESS
DANIEL WRAY
GILAD YAKOV
DANAH YASSIN
MAY YASSIN
DANIEL YEFET
JOANNA YEFET

HARRY CHAN
SOPHIE HAWKEY-EDWARDS
REBECCA KATREIN
DANIEL KESSLER
CLAUDIA MASSEY
ALI MOHANNA
STUART ROWE
NATHANIEL SCHOOLER
SUFIAN AL-MUKHTAR
DAVID BRIM
JAMES BUSSELL
SEBASTIAN CHANDER
TERRELL COLE
NINO CONSTANTINI
DANIELLE CROMPTON
DIMITRIS EFTHIMIOU
ANTIONETTE FERNANDEZ
TAMARA FOGLE
FEISEL GWADERI
ARRIANA HOHENLOHE
NICHOLAS JOHNSON
NATALIE KADAS
REBECCA KATREIN
EMILLE KHADER
BIBI KERVALIAN
MARINA LIVANOS
AISHA McKENZIE
JENNNIFER McNEICE
WILLIAM MILLS
CHRISTINA RITTER
DANIEL WESTON

**YEAR 1980**
SHAYMA AL-MASHAT
SUFIAN AL-MUKHTAR
LUJO BAUER
BARON BLOOM
BEVERLEY BLOOM
DAVID BRIM
JAMES BUSSELL
SEBASTIAN CHANDER
RHONA CLELLAND
TERRELL COLE
NINO CONSTANTINI
DANIELLE CROMPTON
SEREEN DAOU
DORIAN DELAP
DIMITRIS EFTHIMIOU
TAMARA FOGLE
ANTIONETTE FERNANDEZ
ALEXANDER GATWOOD
RAMI CHANDOUR
NICHOLAS GINSBERG
MIRANDA GLASSER
SAM GORDON
DAVID HAYDEN
SOPHIA HENG

136

STEFAN HANANIA
ARRIANA HOHENLOHE
FLETCHER HOROBIN
NICHOLAS JOHNSON
NATALIE KADAS
REBECCA KATREIN
BIBI KERVALIAN
TALAL KHAWAJA
PETER LAWN
LUKE LEANDER
RUDOLF LEANDER
MARIKA LEMOS
XENIA LEMOS
MARINA LIVANOS
KATE LOUSTAU-LALANNE
OLIVER LUROT
CLAUDIA MASSEY
POLLY McCOWEN
AISHA McKENZIE
JENNIFER McNEICE
WILLIAM MILLS
LEE MOHLERE
ALEXANDER NIX
MARK PARKINSON
TAYMOUR POLDING
GENNA PRESTON
CHRISTINA RITTER
STUART ROWE
NATHANIEL SCHOOLER
MAXWELL SHILLINGLAW
JULIAN SOPER
ROBERT SOPER
MAYA TAYARA
ALEXANDRA TOWNSLEY
SIMON VASCO
BRENDAN WALSH
DANIEL WESTON
DANAH YASSIN
MAY YASSIN
NORA YASSIN
TARIQ AL-KHATER
MILAN CORCORAN
ANASTASIA FEIFER
RHODA KAPOOR
EMILLE KHADER
HARLEY McKINLEY
THOMAS NORCLIFFE
KATY ROTH
RUPERT WILLATS
SAMER BARRAGE
TANIA BIJLANI
KUNAL BIJLANI
JOSHUA GRAY
ANGUS HILLEARY
TALAL KHAWAJA
JENNIFER KAYE
ROSS LOCKHART

TOBY MILLER
ALENA POLEMIS
RICHARD PRICE
MAX ROBINSON
NICHOLAS SINGH
SHALINA VARMA
NAZAR YASIN
SANDRA ZOUAKA

**YEAR 1981**
TARIQ AL-KHATAR
SHAYMA AL-MASHAT
HAMID AMIRANI
FELICITY ANDERSON-LYNES
SAMER BARRAGE
LEISHA BRACE
DAVID BRIM
JAMES BUSSELL
ALEXANDER CAIN
SEBASTIAN CHANDER
MILAN CORCORAN
DANIELLE CROMPTON
POPPY EDWARDS
DIMITRIS EFTHIMIOU
YUSUF EL-ANSARI
NICHOLAS GINSBERG
ANNEMARIE GORMAN
JOSHUA GRAY
NIKOLAS HALPER
STEFAN HANANIA
KIM HARRIS
ANGUS HILLEARY
NICHOLAS JOHNSON
NATALIE KADAS
RADHA KAPOOR
TALAL KHAWAJA
RUDOLF LEANDER
ROSS LOCKHART
MARINA LIVANOS
JENNIFER KAYE
CLAUDIA MASSEY
NICOLA MARCEL
AISHA McKENZIE
HARLEY McKINLEY
TOBY MILLER
WILLIAM MILLS
LEE MOHLERE
THOMAS NORCLIFFE
ALINA POLEMIS
RICHARD PRICE
CHRISTINA RITTER
MAX ROBINSON
KATIE ROTH
STUART ROWE
MORAD SALMANPOUR
JACQUES SCHOOLER
NICOLAS SINGH

LOUISE SORENSEN
ALEXANDRA TOWNSLEY
SIMON VASCO
DANIEL WESTON
RUPERT WILLATS
SANDRA ZOVAK
NASSER AL-KATAR
LORENZO DI BELLO CENCI
TAREK ELAWADI
IMAN EL-GHARIB
CLAIRE GLORNEY
TURGET GUNERI
JACK HUSSEIN
EMILE KHADER
MELANIE WESTON
PASCAL YEFET
FELICITY ANDERSON-LYNES
SASHA BRENNER
MICHAEL BRIM
ZAYLIE BUSSELL
TARUM BUXANI
AYMERIC BUCHER
FIONA CAMERON
LAURA GIBSON
RICHARD GIBSON
PETRONELLA GORDON-DEAN
ELIZABETH HANNIFFY
JONATHAN HARVEY
SARA JAMES
ROBIN KAY
KALLIOPI LEMOS
SERENA MATTAR
FRANCES MOFFAT
KIMBERLEY MORGAN
HELENE SYKES
VICTORIA STONE
GEORGINA TOWNSLEY
DAPHNE VALAMBOUS
JANE WARWICK
TIMOTHY WOODCOCK

**YEAR 1982**
NASSER AL-KATAR
NOOR ANSARI
DINA ANDREANIS
LEISHA BRACE
SASHA BRENNER
DAVID BRIM
MICHAEL BRIM
ZAYLIE BUSSELL
BETH BUTTON
TARUN BUXANI
ALEXANDER CAIN
MILAN CORCORAN
FIONA CAMERON
LORENZO DI BELLO CENCI
DAVINA CHEETHAM-SALIK

DANIELLE CROMPTON
BETTINA DAVIDSON
POPPY EDWARDS
YUSEF EL-ANSARI
IMAN EL-GHARIB
RICHARD GIBSON
LAURA GIBSON
CLAIRE GLORNEY
PETRONELLA GORDON-DEAN
ANNEMARIE GORMAN
NICHOLAS GINSBERG
TURGET GURNET
NICHOLAS HALPER
ELIZABETH HANNIFY
JOHNATHAN HARVEY
ANGUS HILLEARY
JACK HUSSEIN
SARAH JAMEEL
ROBIN KAYE
JENNIFER KAYE
KALIOPI LEMOS
ROSS LOCKHART
SERENA MATTAR
TOBY MILLER
FRANCES MOFFAT
KIMBERLEY MORGAN
LEE MOHLERE
THOMAS NORCLIFFE
ALINA POLEMIS
KATIE ROTH
JACQUES SCHOOLER
HELEN SKINAS
NICHOLAS SINGH
VICTORIA STONE
GABRIELLE TARRANT
GEORGINA TOWNSLEY
ALEXANDER TOWNSLEY
DAPHNE VALAMBOUS
JANE WARWICK
DANIEL WESTON
MELANIE WESTON
CONSTANTINA ANDREADIS
BETTINA DAVIDSON
BENJAMIN HOWARD
JARENE THEUNISSEN
REBECCA WADE
LUCY WIGRAM
TOMI ADEMOLA
TITI ADEMOLA
JORGE ALARIO
NANCY FARMY
CATHERINE FOROUGHI
JOEL GAZDAR
AYMERIC BUCHER
ALEXANDER CAIN
EDWARD WATTS

MICHAEL ZOLOTAS
MARION POLDING

**YEAR 1983**
TITI ADEMOLA
TOMI ADEMOLA
FAIZAL ALAUDDIN
CONSTANTINA ANDREADIS
JORGE ALARIO
PAUL BECCI
SASHA BRENNER
VICTORIA BURTON
LOUISE BUTLER
ZAYLIE BUSSELL
MICHAEL BRIM
YASMINA ASSEILY
TORI CARDOSA
LORENZO DI BELLO CENCI
DAVINA CHEETHAM-SAKLIK
ATEH DAMACHI
BETTINA DAVIDSON
SAMUEL DYMOND
POPPY EDWARDS
ADHAM EL-GHARBI
NANCY FARMY
CATHERINE FOROUGHI
JOEL GAZDAR
RICHARD GIBSON
CLAIRE GLORNEY
PETRONELLA GORDON-DEAN
MIRANDA HAFEZ
KIM HARRIS
BENJAMIN HOWARD
JOSHUA KETTLE
DAISY LE VAY
KALLIOPI LEMOS
NATHALIE LOCKTON
GABRIEL MARKSON
SERENA MATTAR
REBECCA MAXWELL
VISHAL MELWANI
AYSEM MONACO
KIMBERLEY MORGAN
GIDEON NEDAS
MARION POLDING
ALINA POLEMIS
LEONIDOS POLEMIS
MARIA PORFYRATOS
MARY POWELL
RICHARD POWELL
ZARA SIDDIQUI
VICTORIA STONE
GABRIELLE TARRANT
JARENE THEUNISSEN
GEORGINA TOWNSLEY
DAPHNE VALAMBOUS
REBECCA WADE

JANE WARWICK
EDWARD WATTS
MELANIE WESTON
LUCY WITHAM
MICHAEL ZOLOTAS
FRANCES MOFFAT
JOANNE MOFFAT
AHMED ALAWADI
ANSEIY ALI
SERAJ DAREK
VIVIENNE CRIAS
OLIVER GLASS
JEANNE HANCOCK
PHILOMENA KEET
DIANA KOOSTRA
AARON MERALI
JACK MERRINGTON
YANNIS VALAMBOUS
NORA BADR
AURORE BELFRAGE
JAMES BRITTON
SARAH FRASURE
VIRGINIA FRASURE
KATIE GLASS
MARKHAM HANSON
JOSEPHINE JACKSON
ADAM KHORSHID
BENJAMIN LINNIT
STAVROS LIVANOS
JENNIFER LJUNGHAMMER
ALI MALIK
GEORGE MANGOS
MARC MUNRO
JOANNE PRESTON
ALEXANDER REDFERN
KERN SCHMID
MARIANNA TRECHAKIS
LLOYD TURNER
GEORGE TZIRAS
CHRISTOPHER WEBLEY

**YEAR 1984**
FAISAL ALLUDIN
ANSEIY ALI
NORA BADR
PAUL BECCI
AURORE BELFRAGE
MICHAEL BRIM
SASHA BRENNER
JAMES BRITTON
VICTORIA BURTON
ZAYLIE BUSSELL
TORI CARDOSA
VIVIENE CRIAS
SAMUEL DYMOND
NANCY FARMY

CATHERINE FOROUGHI
SARAH FRASURE
VIRGINIA FRASURE
JOEL GAZDAR
KATIE GLASS
OLIVER GLASS
CLAIRE GLORNEY
RICHARD GIBSON
JEANNE HANCOCK
MARKHAM HANSON
BENJAMIN HOWARD
JOSEPHINE JACKSON
PHILOMENA KEET
ADAM KHORSHID
DIANA KOOSTRA
DAISY LE VAY
BENJAMIN LINNIT
STAVROS LIVANOS
NATHALIE LOCKTON
JENNIFER LJUNGHAMMER
ALI MALIK
GEORGE MANGOS
REBECCA MAXWELL
GABRIEL MARKSON
AARON MERALI
JACK MERRINGTON
JOANNE MOFFAT
AYSEM MONACO
MARC MUNRO
GIDEON NEDAS
MARIA PORFRYRATOS
RICHARD POWELL
LEONADIS POLEMIS
JOANNE PRESTON
ALEXANDER REDFERN
KERN SCHMID
ZARA SIDDIQUI
GEORGINA TOWNSLEY
MARIANNA TRECHAKIS
LLOYD TURNER
GEORGE TZIRAS
CHRISTOPHER WEBLEY
SARA DAVIES
STEVEN GARCIA
JAMES JENKINS
JEMIMA KEY
JOSHUA LEHMANN
EDWARD WATTS
MELANIE WESTON
SAMEER DALAMAL
SAFINAZ EL-ANSARI
JO JO JACKSON
DANIA MURERWA
KARIM SULTAN
SHARON TAN
VERONICA VASCO
ALEXANDER VERZARIU

YANNIS VALAMBOUS
NOFEL AL-ABDULALY
EDWARD BALFOUR
CAMILLA BATES
PRINCE BAHAR BOLKAIH
TENI CARDOSA
DREW CONROY
EMMA DAVIES
JAMES ELDERTON
ADHAM EL-GHARIB
JAMES HARRIS
REBECCA MILLER
DINA NAWBAR
CAMILLA NOBLE-WARREN
CHARLOTTE PARKER
TROY POTTER
CY ELLIOTT SMITH
JAMES THEUNISSEN
MARC SODHY
PHILIPPA SOSKIN


**YEAR 1985**
NOFEL AL-ABDULALY
DANA AL-KUTOUBI
LUKE ARCHER-NOLAN
NORA BADR
EDWARD BALFOUR
CAMILLA BATES
PRINCE BAHAR BOLKIAH
DREW CONROY
VIVIENNE CRIAS
CY ELLIOTT SMITH
JAMES ELDERTON
STEVEN GARCIA
JAMES HARRIS
JADE HOPE
NAOMI ISMAIL
TANYA ISRANI
JO-JO JACKSON
JAMES JENKINS
JEMIMA KEY
MONA KHAN
PHILOMENA KEET
DIANA KOOSTRA
KAREN LAW
JOSHUA LEHMANN
BETTY MAMOUD
RAMSEY MAMOUD
GABRIEL MARKSON
MATTHEW McFARLANE
AARON MERALI
LAMIA MOWAD
HOLA MOWAD
REBECCA MILLER
JOANNE MOFFATT
PHILIP MOORE
DANIA MURERWA

MARC MUNRO
DIMA NAWBAR
CAMILLA NOBLE-WARREN
CHARLOTTE PARKER
TROY POTTER
MARIA PORFYRATOS
RICHARD POWELL
JOANNA PRESTON
ALEXANDER REDFERN
ALASTAIR ROWE
KERN SCHMID
MARC SODHY
KARIM SULTAN
JARENE THEUNISSEN
LLOYD TURNER
MARIANNA TRECHAKIS
GEORGE TIRAS
CHRISTOPHER WEBLEY
ANTHONY WHITEHEAD
AHMED AL-BASRY
KRISTON ANDON
ADHAM EL-GHARIB
SAFINAZ EL-ANSARI
KATIE GLASS
HARRY KEY
ANGELA LEMOS
CHRISTOPHER RILEY
RAINE RIMMER
INSHA RIZA
CARLY RUNCORN
JAMES THEINNISSEN
ASHLEY TANNER
MARIANNA TZOUMARAS
SARA FAKIH
EDDIE ALBASRY
YASMIN ALBASRY
TAIMUR AL-SAID
EDWARD BRAUNE
CHESTER CHIPPERFIELD
HENRY EMBLETON
TARIQ FARMY
LILY GOSCHEN
SARAH HAMMOND
KATHERINE HARDY
WAEL ITANI
KARIM ITANI
ANDREW JAZARLI
NATASHA KILBY
MAXIMILLIAN LEHMANN
JONATHAN MILLET
STEPHANIE MASHOR
SARAH OSMAN
JOSHUA POLLEN
ALEXANDER SAGE
ZARA SIDDIQUI
NICOLE TALREJA
VANESSA WOZNIAK

SIMBA MURERWA
HEBET YOUSUF
SAMEER YOUSUF

## YEAR 1986

REZA ABDULLA
EDDIE ALBASRY
YASMIN ALBASRY
RONKE ADEYEYE
KRISTON ANDON
CAMILLA BATES
EDWARD BRAUNE
CHESTER CHIPPERFIELD
DREW CONROY
ALEXANDER DELMONT
CY ELLIOTT SMITH
HENRY EMBLETON
TARIQ FARMY
NATASHA GABEL
KATHERINE HARDY
JAMES HARRIS
JADE HOPE
KARIM ITANI
WAEL ITANI
TANYA ISRANI
MONA KHAN
NATASHA KILBY
ANDREW JAZARLI
TROY POTTER
KARIN LAW
JOSHUA LEHMANN
MAX LEHMANN
RAMSEY MAHOUD
STEPHANIE MASHOR
MATTHEW McFARLANE
MARK MANDUCA
JONATHAN MILLET
MARC MUNRO
DIMA NAWBAR
CAMILLA NOBLE WARREN
SARAH OSMAN
ALASTAIR ROWE
CARLY RUNCORN
DYALA RODA
MARY EL-SAID
ALEXANDER SAGE
ELLIOT SCHMID
ZARA SIDDIQUI
MONA SIDDIQUI
KIMI TAKEBAYASHI
NICOLE TALREGA
JAMES THEUNISSEN
ANTHONY WHITEHEAD
VANESSA WOZNIAK
SHAKTHI VIJAYAKUMA
SAMEER YOUSUF
HEBET YOUSUF

HABBY ZAINIDI
GADAH AL-ABDULALY
DANA AL-KUTOUBI
JAMES GABEL
FARAH HAMEED
ASHLEY TANNER
TIMOTHY WHITEHEAD
SITI YUSOF
DINA AMIN
FRANCES BRAUNE
SABRINA CURRIMBHOY
ALEXIA DHRUVE
LUCY EDWARDS
RUFUS GORDON DEAN
CHARLES JENKINS
ALASTAIR JESSOP
ROXANNA KONG
ANNABELLE LEHAVRE
MARK McLEISH
TANIA NAWBAR
SHERIF OMAN
JAMES PROFUMO
KATIE SIMPSON
TANIA SODHY
KIMI TAKEBAYASHI
GAVIN TUCKER
ALEXANDER VALDES

**YEAR 1987**
DIMA AMIN
SARA AMIN
JUAN ARROYA
ALEXANDER BAIRD
CAMILLA BATES
EDWARD BRAUNE
PANCHETA BRAUNE
ADAM BUTTERFIELD
ALEXANDER BURTON
CHESTER CHIPPERFIELD
ALEXANDER DELMONT
ALEX DHRUVE
LUCY EDWARDS
HENRY EMBLETON
JAMES GABEL
RUFUS GORDON DEAN
HIND HABIB
DANIEL HARRIS
ALISTAIR JESSOP
CHARLES JENKINS
OMAR KHAN
NATASHA KILBY
ANNABELLE LE HAVRE

MONICA LARKIN
MAX LEHMANN
DOMINIC MASON
MARK McLEISH
MARK MANDUCA
JONATHAN MILLET
RANWA OBEID
TANIA NAWBAR
SHERIFF OSMAN
JAMES PROFUMO
ALASTAIR ROWE
CARLY RUNCORN
KIMBERLEY SALMON
ELLIOT SCHMID
HUMZA SIDDIQUI
KATIE SIMPSON
TANYA SODHY
KIMI TAKEBAYASHI
NICOLE TALREJA
ASHLEY TANNER
TIM TOMKINSON
GAVIN TUCKER
ALEXANDER VALDES
TIMOTHY WHITEHEAD
VANESSA WOZNIAK
SAMEER YUSOF
HABBY ZAINIDI
SABRINA CURRIMBHOY
ROXANNA KONG
OSCAR DUFFY
BASIL KRONFLI
WALEED ALAWI
ABDUL ALAWI
NOOF AL-KHATANI
JAMES BROWN
ENRICO CIVIDINO
EMMA DAVIES
LAURA DOWSETT
SARA JABER
ANN HUSSIN
MELISSA MALLEY
STEPHEN MICHELINI
JACK POWELL
CHARLOTTE RADCLIFFE
SEAN RAJANAKE
CAROLINE RODRIGUES
CELINE REDFERN
FAY ROBINSON
RACHEL SIM
SARAH REITH
FIONA TAN
ALEXANDER VALDES

# APPENDIX 2

ALPHABETICAL INDEX

BARDSLEY, Clare
BARETTO, Mark
BARNETT, Joanna
BARNETT, Sarah
BARRAGE, Samer
BARROS, Rodolfo
BARROS, Jan Miguel
BATES, Camilla
BATTENFIELD, Brenton
BAUER, Leijo
BAYARIA, Rajiv
BEAN, David
BEAVERS, Rosalind
BECKMAN, Robert
BECCI, Juan
BEDACK, Oliver
BEDFORD, Piers
BEEBER, Alexander
BEGGIATO, Sergio
BEINDORFF, Caroline
BEINDORFF, Nicola
BEITNER, Nicolas
BELFRAGE, Aurore
BENNETT, Victoria
BERBAKOFF, Michele
BERGER, Charles
BERLIN, Melanie
BERLIN, Philip
BERQUIST, James
BERRY, Anne
BERRY, Margaret
BESKER, Lujo
BETHELL, James
BETHELL, William
BHAI, Kadijah
BIDDLE, Jane
BIJLANI, Sunal
BIJLANI, Tania
BIRNHAK, Laura
BIRNHAK, Martin
BOLKIAH, Prince Bahar
BLACK, Emily
BLOOM, Baron
BLOOM, Beverly
BLUETT, Marcus
BOURGEOIS, Etienne
BOURGEOIS, Patrick
BOURGEOIS, Veronique
BOURNE, Emma
BOURNE, Nicholas
BOWEN, Christopher
BOWEN, Joanna
BRACE, Leisha
BRADSTOCK, Deborah
BRADY, Hope
BRAUNE, Alexander
BRAUNE, Edward

BRAUNE, Lucilla
BRAUNE, Pancheta
BREITMEYER, Geoffrey
BRENER, Fleur
BRENNER, Joshua
BRENNER, Matthew
BRENNER, Sasha
BRESLER, Katherine
BRESLER, Nicholas
BRESLER, Nicole
BRICHTO, Anne
BRIGGS, Jason
BRIGGS, Paul
BRIM, David
BRIM, Michael
BRITTON, James
BRODER, Rebecca
BROOKE, Alexander
BROVAT, Tamara
BROWN, Helen
BROWN, Henry
BROWN, Jocelyn
BROWN, John
BRYANT, Charles
BRYANT, Sarah
BUCHER, Aymeric
BUCSI, Carolyn
BUDDEN, Andrew
BULL, Peter
BUNYAN, Rebecca
BURNETT, Daniel
BURNETT, Simon
BURTON, Alexander
BURTON, Victoria
BUSSELL, James
BUSSELL, Zaylie
BUTTON, Beth
BUTLER, Grant
BUTLER, Louise
BUXANI, Tarun
BUXANI, Amereeta
BYNER, Anne


C
CAIN, Alexander
CALVO, Suzanna
CAMERON, Fiona
CANNON, David
CAPE, Jonathan
CARDOSO, Teni
CARDOSO, Tori
CARNEGIE, Alexandra
CEARNS, Jeremy
CHAN, Cedrych
CHAN, Harry
CHANDARIA, Aanal

145

ELDERTON, James
EL GHARIB, Adham
EL-GHARIB, Iman
EL-HALAB, Natalie
ELLE, Rhona
ELLIOTT, Daniel
ELLIOTT, Joshua
ELLIOTT-SMITH, Cy
ELSAESSER, Anna
EL SAID, Mary
EL SAID, Rowina Ann
EL-SALEH, Fatma
EMBLETON, Henry
ENGLISH, Rupert
ENVERGA, Rosalie
ERYANI, Amar
EVANS, Christopher

**F**

FABRICANT, Mary
FAIMAN, Jonathan
FAKIM, Sara
FANCY, Tareq
FARAH, Camilla
FARMY, Nancy
FARR, Amber
FARR, Dylan
FARR-LEANDER, Luke
FAVRE, Isabelle
FAYE, Anthony
FEDESKI, John
FEDESKI, Tina
FEIFER, Anastasia
FEIFER, Gresha
FELLOWS, Charles
FELLOWS, James
FERNANDEZ, Antoinette
FERNANDEZ, Maria
FLACCOMIO, Philip
FOGLE, Tamara
FORBES, Aaron
FORBES, Jessica
FOREMAN, Amanda
FOREMAN, Jonathan
FORSANDER, Elisabeth
FOSTER, Mary
FOX, Fenella
FOXON, David
FRANCIS, Darren
FRANCIS, Jordan
FRASER, Joanna
FRASURE, Sarah
FRASURE, Virginia
FREEDMAN, Jonathan
FREEMAN, Benjamin
FREEMAN, Lee

FROST, Annabel
FROST, Georgina
FROST, Victoria
FRY, Lisa
FURLOUGH, Catherine

**G**

GABB, Owen
GABEL, Natasha
GAETZ, Susan
GALATIS, Nicolas
GALSBERG, Susan
GARCIA, Nicole
GARCIA, Steven
GARCIA-NEILSON, Camelia
GARDNER-BROWN, Richard
GARFIELD, Scott
GARFIELD, Tracy
GARRARD, Hannah
GATWARD, Alexander
GATWARD, Tamara
GAZDAR, Joel
GEHA, Michael
GERMING, Anne
GESUA, Rachel
GHANDOUR, Rami
GHANDOUR, Talal
GIBSON, Laura
GIBSON, Richard
GILRAIN, Kevin
GILRAIN, Mark
GILROY, Fergus
GILROY, Margaret
GILMAN, Kathleen
GINSBERG, David
GINSBERG, Nicholas
GLASGOE, Emma
GLASGOE, Kate
GLASS, Kate
GLASS, Oliver
GLASSER, Miranda
GLASSER, Roland
GLORNAY, Claire
GOATER, Anne
GOATER, Mark
GOHARIAN, Roxanna
GOLD, Claire
GOLD, Daniel
GOLD, Melanie
GOLD, Nicholas
GOLDING, Natalie
GOLDRING, Joanne
GOLDSMITH, Alex
GONSHAW, Justine
GONSHAW, Penelope
GOODMAN, Diana
GOODRICK, Simon

INGHAM, Donald
INGLIS, Neil
IOANNOU, Christos
IOANNOU, Maria
IPALE, Daniel
IRAOLA, Michelle
IRVINE, David
ISMAIL, Mona
ISMAIL, Naomi
ISRANI, Tanya
ITANI, Karim
ITANI, Wael
IVANOVIC, Lara


**J**

JABER, Sara
JACKMAN, Elizabeth
JACKSON, Jo Jo
JACKSON, Nicolas
JACOBS, David
JAIN, Jagrati
JAIN, Saandeer
JAMBO, Saddiq
JAMES, Lucy
JAMES, Sarah
JARADE, Gabriella
JAZARLI, Andrew
JENKINS, Charles
JENKINS, James
JENKINS, Lillie
JESSOP, Alistair
JOACHIM, John
JODRELL, Henry
JOHNS, Matthew
JOHNS, Simon
JOHNSON, Amy
JOHNSON, Andrea
JOHNSON, Emily
JOLYON, Luke
JONES, David
JOSEPH, Heidi
JOSEPH, Kate
JOSEPH, Lisa
JUDSON, Thomas
JUNDI, Sophia


**K**

KADAS, Natalie
KAHNE, Inger
KALAYDJIAN, Sarkis
KAMALI, Karim
KANEKO, Nina
KAPOOR, Radha
KARKI, Johnne
KASTNER, Dillon

KASTNER, Milicia
KATAOKA, Hiroshi
KATO, Katy
KATREIN, Rebecca
KAY, Robin
KAY, Wendy
KAYE, Jennifer
KAYOAKA, Susuma
KAZOLIDES, Nadia
KEARNS, Jeremy
KEEFE, Brian
KEEFE, Heather
KEENAN, Sarah
KEET, Philomena
KELLY, Daniel
KELLY, Heather
KELLY, Jonathan
KELLY, Rick
KENNEDY, David
KER-LINDSAY, James
KER-LINDSAY, Mark
KERVALIAN, Bibi
KERSERUANI, James
KERSERUANI, Joe
KESSLER, Daniel
KESSLER, Edward
KESSLER, Mark
KETTLE, Joshua
KEY, Harry
KEY, Jemima
KHADAR, Emile
KHALILI, Mustafa
KHALILI, Walid
KHAN, Oman
KHAN, Shujon
KHASHOGGI, Nabila
KHAWAJA, Aizeh
KHAWAJA, Kaisal
KHAWAJA, Talal
KHORSHID, Adam
KIKANO, Mark
KING, Polly
KINROSS, Charles
KINROSS, Katherine
KISH, Karen
KITCHEN, Carl-Christian
KLEONAKOS, Alexia
KLONARIS, Michael
KONG, Roanna
KONIALIDIS, Alexandra
KONIALIDIS, Nicholas
KOOTSTRA, Diana
KOPLEY, Austen
KOPLEY, Barbara
KOPLEY, Rebecca
KOTTNAUER, Daniella
KRONFLI, Basil

149

MALLINSON, Roland
MALLINSON, Rosanna
MALLINSON, Sheila
MALMGREN, Lance
MAMOUD, Betty
MAMOUD, Ramsay
MANDUCA, Mark
MANGOS, George
MANLEY, Peter
MARCEL, Camilla
MARCEL, Nicola
MARGOLIS, George
MARGOLIS, Rachel
MARKS, Julian
MARKSON, Gabriel
MARQUEZ, Rodrigo
MARQUEZ, Lynette
MARTELL, Charlotte
MARTIN, Javier
MASELLA, Maria
MASHOR, Stephanie
MASON, Dominic
MASON, Rebecca
MASON, Vanessa
MASSEY, Alexander
MASSEY, Claudia
MASSOT, Jason
MASTERS, Lara
MATSUNOBE, June
MATTAR, Serena
MAXWELL, Rebecca
MELAMED, John
MELWANI, Anil
MELWANI, Vishal
MENMUIR, Anna
MENNINI, Chiara
MERALI, Aaron
MERRINGTON, Jack
MEYER, Amanda
MEYER, Anthony
MEYER, Joanna
MICHAELS, Mark
MICHAELS, Mary
MIDGEN, Jacqueline
MILLER, Amanda
MILLER, Rebecca
MILLER, Toby
MILLET, Jonathan
MILLS, William
MITCHELL, Michael
MITFORD, Emma
MITFORD, Henrietta Jane
MITFORD, Georgina
MITFORD, Kate
MITFORD, Rupert
MITFORD, Tessa
MITFORD, Victoria Louise

MOAWAD, Hola
MOAWAD, Lamia
MODET, Alisa
MODET, Paul
MODY, Eleanor
MOFFAT, Frances
MOFFAT, Joanne
MOHANNA, Ali
MOHARAM, Ahmed
MOHLERE, Lee
MONACO, Aysem
MONDANI, Waleed
MONSEAU, Florence
MONTGOMERY, Kay
MOORE, Philip
MORGAN, Kimberley
MORRISON, Gabriel
MORRISON, Rupert
MOSS, Alison
MOUDARI, Louise
MOULTING, Meg
MOXHAM, Tiffany
MRUCK, Sabina
MUIR, Edward John
MULLINS, Jane
MULLINS, Mark
MUNRO, Amy
MUNRO, Mark
MURDOCK, Andrew
MURDOCK, Elisabeth
MURERWA, Dania
MURERWA, Simba
MYERS, Nicholas


N
NABULIS, Radi
NAIR, Deepa
NARANAIPGNI, Dashi
NASH, Justin
NAWBAR, Dima
NAWBAR, Tanya
NEDAS, Gideon
NEWLEY, Sasha
NEWLEY, Tara
NEWTON, John
NG, Kalina
NIKOLAOU, Christina
NILSEN, Laura
NIX, Alexander
NIX, Samantha
NOBLE-WARREN, Camilla
NOGUCHI, Yoko
NORCLIFFE, Thomas
NOTT, Michael
NUZZO, Mario

ROMANO, Lisa
RONEY, Juliet
ROSSDALE, Gavin
ROSSDALE, Loraine
ROTH, Katie
ROTHGIESSER, Andrew
ROWE, Alastair
ROWE, Stuart
RUNCORN, Carly
RUSSELL, Robin, Lord
RYKWERT, Sebastian

**S**
SAATCHI, Edward
SADAK, Philip
SAGE, Alexander
SAKELLARIOS, Emanuel
SAKELLARIOS, Manolis
SALEH, Nihal
SALMANPOUR, Kayvan
SALMON, Kimberley
SALVATORI, Natalie
SAMAHA, Marilyn
SAMAHA, Nancy
SANDERSON, Sarah
SASSOON, David
SASSON, Robert
SATURNINUS, Louise
SAUNDERS, Kate
SAVARESE, Simon
SCHOOLER, Jacques
SCHOOLER, Nathaniel
SCHRODER, Leonie
SCHMID, Elliot
SCHMID, Kern
SELLAR, Paul
SERVAES, Mark
SESSLER, Simon
SHAH, Vimi
SHAH, Vishesh
SHAMIS, Rania
SHAND-KYDD, Casper
SHAND-KYDD, Lucy
SHARP, Fabian
SHARP, Leonore
SHASHOUR, Daniel
SHEPARD, Giles
SHEPARD, Tara,
SHILLINGLAW, Maxwell
SHOUCAIR, Geno
SIDDIQUI, Humza
SIDDIQUI, Mona
SIDDIQUI, Zara
SIEFF, Jonathan
SIEFF, Patrick
SIEFF, Simon

SIM, Camilla
SIM, Rachel
SIMKIN, Luke
SIMMONDS, Jason
SIMMONDS, Tristan
SIMPSON, Amanda
SIMPSON, Jason
SIMPSON, Katherine
SINCLAIR, Kelly
SINGH, Nicholas
SINGH, Tekla
SODHY, Marc
SODHY, Tania
SOFAIR, Danya
SOFAIR, Oved
SOLOMONS, Laura
SOPER, Julian
SOPER, Robert
SOPER, David
SORENSEN, Louise
SOSKIN, Philippa
SOUFRAKI, Sahavet
SPAR, Alexandra
SREIH, Sarah
SPIERS, Sally
SPIERS, Sarah
SPOONER, Adrian
ST. CLAIR, Colette
ST. GEORGE, Christopher
ST. GEORGE, David
STAINSBY, Polly Jane
STANDER, Eve
STANLEY JONES, Charlotte
STANLEY JONES, Nicholas
STANWAY, Charles
STEIN, Paula
STEINER, Karl
STELLAKIS, Cynthia
STEWART, Fiona
STEWART-WILSON, Alice
STONE, Deborah
STONE, Sara
STONE, Victoria
STONEMAN, Sarah
STRATTON, Rupert
STRATTON CHRISTIANSON,
  Juliana
STRATTON CHRISTIANSON,
  Justin
STRAUSS, James
STRAUSS, Toby
SWANEPOEL, Angelique
SULTAN, Akram
SULTAN, Karim
SUPER, David
SWINEY, Sophie
SWINEY, Suzette

WILKINSON, Marcus
WILLATS, Holly
WILLATS, Rupert
WILLIAMS, Andrew
WILLIAMS, Julian
WILLIAMS, Timothy
WILLIAMS, Toby
WITHAM, Lucy
WOLFSON, Deborah
WOODCOCK, Timothy
WOODIWISS, Ben
WOODMAN, Amanda
WOODMAN, Simon
WOZNIAK, Vanessa
WRAY, Daniel

**Y**
YAKOV, Gilad
YASSIN, Danah

YASSIN, May
YASSIN, Nora
YEFET, Daniel
YEFET, Joanna
YOUSUF, Hebet
YOUSUF, Sameer
YUSOF, Ambereen
YUSOF, Siti
YUSOF, Zeffriali

**Z**
ZAHLER, Alexander
ZAINIDI, Habby
ZERVUDACHI, Laky
ZERVUDACHI, Patrick
ZOLOTAS, Michael
ZOBEL-DE-AYALA, Monica Sofia
ZOVAK, Sandra